KNOWING CHRISTIANITY

CHRISTIANITY: A PSYCHOLOGIST'S
TRANSLATION

KNOWING CHRISTIANITY

A series edited by Dr. William Neil to provide for thinking laymen a solid but non-technical presentation of what the Christian religion is and what it has to say.

The first titles are:

THE CHRISTIAN FAITH	F. W. Dillistone
THE OLD TESTAMENT	Robert Davidson
THE LIFE AND TEACHING OF JESUS	William Neil
GOD IN THE NEW TESTAMENT	A. W. Argyle
THE EARLY CHURCH	W. H. C. Frend
FAITH AND PHILOSOPHY	J. Richmond
CHRISTIANITY AND OTHER RELIGIONS	E. O. James
THE CHRISTIAN FATHERS	Maurice Wiles
THE ATONEMENT	F. R. Barry
CHRISTIAN ETHICS	David H. C. Read
THE ROOTS OF THE RADICAL THEOLOGY	John Charles Cooper
CHRISTIAN APOLOGETICS	J. K. S. Reid

KNOWING CHRISTIANITY

CHRISTIANITY: A PSYCHOLOGIST'S TRANSLATION

by

A. T. Welford, M.A., SC.D.

Professor of Psychology in the University of Adelaide.
Formerly Fellow and Chaplain of St. John's College, Cambridge.

HODDER AND STOUGHTON
LONDON SYDNEY AUCKLAND TORONTO

Printed in Great Britain for Hodder and Stoughton Limited, St. Paul's House, Warwick Lane, London, E.C.4 by Ebenezer Baylis and Son Limited, The Trinity Press, Worcester, and London

Editor's Preface

To judge by the unending flow of religious literature from the various publishing houses there is an increasingly large demand on the part of ordinary intelligent people to know more about what Christianity has to say. This series is designed to help meet this need and to cater for just this kind of people.

It assumes there is a growing body of readers, inside and outside the Church, prepared to give serious attention to the nature and claims of the Christian faith, and who expect to be given by theologians authoritative and up-to-date answers to the kind of questions thinking people want to ask.

More and more it becomes clear that we are unlikely to get any answers that will satisfy the deepest needs of the human spirit from any other quarter. Present-day science and philosophy give us little help on the ultimate questions of human destiny. Social, political and educational panaceas leave most of us unpersuaded. If we are not to end our quest for the truth about ourselves and the world we live in in cynicism and disillusionment where else can we turn but to religion.

Too often in the past two thousand years the worst advertisement for Christianity has been its supporters and advocates. Yet alone of all the great world religions it has shown that a faith which was oriental in origin could be transplanted into the Western world and from there strike root again in the East. The present identification of Christianity in the minds of Asians and Africans with European culture and Western capitalism or imperialism is a passing phase. To say that no other religion has the same potentialities as a world-wide faith for everyman is neither to denigrate the God-given truth in Buddhism, Islam and the rest, nor to say that at this stage Christianity as generally practised and understood in the West presents much more than a caricature of its purpose.

Perhaps the best corrective to hasty judgement is to measure these two thousand years against the untold millions of years of man's development. Organised Christianity is still in its infancy, as is the mind of man as he seeks to grapple with truths that could only come to him by revelation. The half has not yet been told and the full implications for human thought and action of the coming of God in Christ have as yet been only dimly grasped by most of us.

It is as a contribution to a deeper understanding of the mystery that surrounds us that this series is offered. The early volumes deal, as is only right, with fundamental issues – the historical impact of Christianity upon mankind based upon its Jewish origins and establishing itself in the wider world; the essence of the Christian faith and the character of Christian behaviour. Later volumes in the series will deal with various aspects of Christian thought and practice in relation to human life in all its variety and with its perennial problems.

The intention is to build up a library which under the general title of "Knowing Christianity" will provide for thinking laymen a solid but non-technical presentation of what the Christian religion is and what it has to say in this atomic age.

The writers invited to contribute to this series are not only experts in their own fields but are all men who are deeply concerned that the gulf should be bridged between the specialised studies of the theologian and the untheologically minded average reader who nevertheless wants to know what theology has to say. I am sure that I speak in the name of all my colleagues in this venture when I express the hope that this series will do much to bridge the gap.

The Univeristy, Nottingham   WILLIAM NEIL

Author's Preface

This book records an attempt to look sympathetically but objectively at Christianity and its present-day tasks, in the light of modern experimental psychology. As a scientist, I should certainly not wish to claim the last word on any of the matters discussed, and recognise that many of the suggestion made, even if they seem plausible now, are likely to be proved wrong or incomplete by subsequent research and events. I have put them forward here because I believe they deserve serious discussion, in the course of which we may hope to arrive at a closer approximation to the truth.

The first two chapters outline some of the main problems with which the psychological study of religion was concerned up to the 1940s — problems mainly of the relationship between religion and psychology, and of the nature and functions of religion in daily life. The third, fourth and fifth chapters deal with the basic Christian concepts of God, conscience, sin, faith and the Church in terms of psychological ideas which were developed mainly during the 1950s and 1960s. The sixth and seventh chapters apply psychological concepts which have grown up in the 1960s to a number of problems with which Christianity has been traditionally concerned, and which are of especial interest today. They include human relationships, both in the family and in the community outside, and the effects of rising population, longevity, affluence and increasingly pervasive social organisation on the quality of life. The final chapter attempts to outline some of the implications of the preceding discussions for the future tasks of Christians and the Church.

The ideas set out in this book have been shaped in discussion with many of my teachers, colleagues, pupils and friends. It would be impossible to acknowledge them all by name, but one must be specially mentioned. Dr. J. S. Boys Smith, while he was my tutor at St. John's, did two things for which I shall always be grateful: first, he took hold of my undergraduate religious questionings and gave them a forward-looking, rational form; and second, he encouraged me to study psychology.

In the actual preparation of this volume, my sincere thanks are due to Mrs. M. Blaber for having excellently performed the difficult task of translating my manuscript into typescript.

Adelaide   A. T. WELFORD
25 May 1970.

Contents

Chapter I

Two Views of Man

Most religious people, if they could put into words what they believed about the fundamental nature of man, would probably say that he was a two-fold being. On the one hand he has a non-material mind and soul which perceives, feels, learns, remembers and initiates action. On the other hand he has a material body which is the vehicle and means of expression for the mind and soul, but is essentially inferior to them. He lives in a world which is largely, although by no means wholly, determined by the physical laws of nature, and this is especially true of his own mental functions. He is free to choose what he does, between good and evil, between important and trivial, between noble and base, and these are conceived as choices between the dictates of the "higher" non-material world of the soul, and the immediacies of physical nature. The task of choosing well is difficult, because man is endowed through heredity and racial history with urges and desires, some of which run counter to the requirements of both worlds, especially the higher. There is thus a continual struggle to control some desires in favour of others which are less immediately insistent, but more important in the long run. Help can be obtained in this struggle, and in coping with the cruel demands of the outside world, by prayer and other religious exercises which align men to the forces of the higher world – forces which must ultimately prove stronger than those of the world of physical nature. Man cannot discover this higher world by his own efforts, but its forces give him glimpses of it by occasionally revealing themselves to him. The various forces, higher and lower, working within man and shaping the course of events in his world, endow each individual differently. Therefore, although one man is like another in many ways, each is nevertheless unique, so that general statements about human beings are hazardous.

Let it be said at once that this is not an expert theologian's view of man. It is stated here because it, or something like it, seems to be widely held and forms the background against which some of the best known statements by psychologists about religion — especially critical statements — have been made.

Until the middle of the nineteenth century, the predominant psychological view of man was in many ways similar. Psychology, then a branch of philosophy, was conceived as the study of the sensations, feelings and acts of will belonging to a conscious mind which, although related to brain and body, was separate from them and "above" them. However, psychology as we know it today had as its parents not only philosophy but also physiology, and in the years since the mid-nineteenth century it has grown progressively away from the first towards the second. In so doing it has moved from a preoccupation with consciousness to the study of behaviour, and became clearly recognised as a branch of biological science.

The modern psychologist's view of man is thus very different from that of most of his philosophical forbears, and even more from that of popular religion. Essentially he regards man as a piece of biological machinery consisting of sense-organs, brain and effectors such as hands and feet. These receive information from the environment, select, codify, order and co-ordinate it, and translate it into action. Information can be stored and used when dealing with subsequent information, so that action is influenced not only by the immediate situation, but by events which have impinged on the organism in the past. As a result, we can often predict future behaviour by looking at the organism's present situation and past history together. In the same way, the organism is able to extrapolate from the present on the assumption that regularities observed in past sequences of events will continue to hold true. It can also deal with new, unfamiliar situations by piecing together information from several different past situations to produce a course of action which is new, in the sense that it does not emerge directly from any one previous experience or action. When this happens, a person may experience a sudden "insight" which seems to come from outside himself in that he cannot introspect the manner of its coming: it is nevertheless clearly the product of his own brain action because it is closely related to the activities and events which preceded it.

Each new situation is dealt with in terms brought from the past, and modifies the information carried forward to the future. The storage of information is thus cumulative and the information in store is always being modified. At the same time, initial dealings with unfamiliar situations are likely to set patterns of response which are repeated when a similar situation recurs. Early experiences thus tend to have longer-lasting and more pervasive effects than those which come later. This has been shown on a short time-scale in many experiments in which the way the task is done the first time seems to determine the way it is done subsequently. It is also implied in the finding that errors made when learning skills such as golf or typewriting, must be corrected at once if they are not to become ingrained, and thus difficult to eliminate later. On a longer time-scale, it is clear that the experiences of early childhood can have profound effects in shaping subsequent personality, interests, attitudes and character.

Drives to action arise not only from environmental circumstances, but from internal physiological states, such as those due to need for food, drink or sexual relief. Such drives tend to be insistent when they occur, and thus often conflict with programmes of action based on wider considerations. In other words, there is often competition between immediate goals based on biological appetites, and longer-term courses of action. Further conflicts and frustrations may arise when the external situation makes unduly heavy demands, leading to stress and fatigue, or makes insufficient demand, so producing monotony and boredom.

The view of man outlined in the last three paragraphs does not deny consciousness, but tries to avoid basing discussion upon it. Behaviour and consciousness are by no means perfectly correlated. For example, excessive demand for effort tends to produce feelings of fatigue, but does not always do so, and feelings of fatigue may occur in the absence of effort. Again, the pallor, sweating, increased heart-rate and other signs of strong emotion are by no means exactly reflected in feelings of anger or fear. The problem therefore arises of whether to deal mainly with behaviour or with consciousness. The modern psychologist tends to choose behaviour for two reasons. Firstly, it is more directly observable and measurable: conscious experience is in an important sense private to the individual, and cannot be directly communicated to others; the best that can be done is to ask the subject to describe his conscious feelings and thoughts, and to treat such descriptions as a form of behaviour, recognising that they may not be completely accurate. Secondly and more important, many mental events are unconscious, so that consciousness gives a seriously incomplete picture of what is shaping an individual's behaviour. The features of a situation which appear in consciousness tend to be those which are rare or unusual, more familiar features being "taken for granted". There is a biological advantage in this being so, since conscious attention is concentrated at those points where reanalysis of a situation and the working out of a new course of action are most needed.

Strictly speaking, the psychologist's view of man leaves no room for free will: man is regarded as an automaton, and his behaviour as entirely the result of his physical constitution, immediate circumstances, and past experience. Here, however, the psychologist finds himself in a dilemma. On the one hand, he knows he must postulate a deterministic model of man if he is to treat human behaviour as lawful; but on the other hand, free will seems to be a fact of experience which any model of man must take into account. Most present-day psychologists resolve this dilemma by taking the determinist view as a working hypothesis in their studies, while tacitly assuming some degree of free will in their practical dealings with other people.

The general line of approach outlined here has, since the 1940s, been carried a stage further by drawing analogies between the human mechanism and various self-regulating machines. Two types especially have been considered. One is the *servo-mechanism*, such as the electronic amplifier with feedback or the ship's power-assisted steering gear, which responds not only to signals coming from the outside, but also to its own activity, so that its overall operation depends on the relationship between these two sources of input. The other type of analogy is with the electronic computer. This, like a human being, combines present input data with previously stored information, according to a "programme" or set of rules determining how the two sources of data shall be used to produce an output dependent on both together.

When drawing such analogies it is not necessary to assume that the actual material and mechanics of the machine—its "hardware"—bear any close resemblance to a human brain: the essential comparison is in terms of the principles and mathematical relationships involved in their operation. In this sense it is fair to challenge anyone who puts forward a psychological theory, to design a machine or write a computer programme that would show the same essential behaviour as human beings if his theory were true. The value of such model-building is that it clarifies the distinctions between different functions or "mechanisms" within the whole system and thus, by analogy, between various basic human capacities and characteristics. Ability and personality can be thought of as depending on both the efficiency of these various mechanisms, and on the way their operation has been programmed as the result of past experience. There is thus plenty of room for unique combinations of capacity and programming in different individuals. At the same time, however, it is possible in principle to analyse the general factors which make up this uniqueness, and so to specify it in general terms.

The psychological and religious views of man that we have outlined, are not as fundamentally opposed as they appear at first sight to be. They differ mainly because they have been developed for different purposes. The psychological view represents a working hypothesis designed to co-ordinate the facts obtained from a large number of scientific studies and to guide the search for further facts. It is thus tentative, subject to frequent modification, and clearly incomplete in that it does not cover areas in which evidence is lacking, such as the nature of administrative skill, political acumen, or intelligence in the ordinary sense of the word as opposed to performance in intelligence tests.

The religious view, on the other hand, aims at co-ordinating the common experience of ordinary men with the special experience of a few and the lessons of history, to provide an orientation towards the world and a guide to everyday life in it. As such it must be complete, in the sense of being able to provide some sort of answer to any question which arises in the course of daily living. The exigencies of moment to moment and day to day will not wait for a solution to be worked out to full scientific standards: man in his ordinary living cannot, like the academic psychologist, suspend judgement if evidence is lacking.

When two parallel systems of ideas have grown up, much can often be learnt from bringing them together. We may well, therefore, advance our understanding of both religion and psychology by looking at each in terms of the other. This we shall try to do in the chapters which follow. In the main we shall be viewing religion in terms of psychology, since it is the latter which now possesses the more detailed knowledge of certain important aspects of man. We shall, however, see that the traffic is by no means wholly one way, and that the study of religion can give some valuable leads to scientific psychology.

PSYCHOLOGICAL APPROACHES TO RELIGION

The lack of fundamental opposition between religious and psychological ideas, and the possibility of both benefiting by their being brought together, has not always been recognised in the past. Religious people have often argued that there is in religion something quite different in quality from the kind of experience or activity with which psychology deals, so that religion cannot come within the scope of psychological enquiry. For example, a psychologist had been reading a paper to a parish society on some of the factors which go to make a balanced personality: afterwards the vicar got up and said, "I don't see why we should not attribute it all to the work of the Holy Spirit *and have done with it*." The fear behind such attitudes appears to be that any rationalising treatment of religion will destroy its emotional content. Many of those who hold this view make the same objection to academic theological studies. Such an argument is both dangerous and false. Emotion unchecked by rational thought is an unreliable guide, leading to sentimentality and inconsistency in one's dealings with people and things. In any case, few artists, musicians or indeed scientists would deny that knowledge tends to refine and sharpen the emotional impact of experience rather than abolish it.

Behind this type of argument there lies, however, a more justifiable suspicion and fear. Those who have attempted to study religion in psychological terms fall broadly into three groups. All three were in different ways influenced by the controversies which arose from the scientific revolution of the nineteenth century. The first of them was openly hostile to religion, and saw psychological study as a means of hastening its destruction. Their argument was, broadly speaking, that since many of the features of religious experience and behaviour appear also in other, non-religious activities of life – for example mystic experiences are often reported with a wealth of sexual metaphor – religion can be *explained away* in terms of normal psychological processes. An early example of this attitude is shown in an experiment by Galton (1908) who put up a comic figure of Punch in his room, invested it in imagination with divine attributes, and found that he eventually acquired something like a religious attitude towards it. Of those who came later, the leading figures were undoubtedly Freud and Leuba. The former pointed out that religious ideas and rituals show similarities to the symptoms of obsessional neurosis. This is true, although it is doubtful whether it is so to such an extent as to warrant Freud's view that religion is to be regarded as a neurosis. He recognised that such similarities did not prove religion to be false, but he held that they rendered it suspect, and looked forward to the day when it would be replaced by science. He seems to have assumed that religious and scientific approaches are irreconcilable, and cannot be, as we suggested earlier, regarded as alternatives, each valid for its own purpose. We shall consider Freud's views in more detail in the next chapter.

Leuba's attitude was simpler and is well expressed in the following quotation:

> Until proof to the contrary is produced, we may set it down that religious experience is made up of the same elements as the rest of conscious life, and that these elements are connected and elaborated according to laws holding for mental life generally.
>
> Expressed in general terms, the task of psychology in respect to the group of facts constituting religious life is to observe, compare, analyze, and to determine the conditions and consequences of the appearing of these facts. Its chief problems . . . may be classified under four heads:
>
> (1) the impulses, motives and aims;
> (2) the means employed to reach the ends – ceremonial, prayer, communion, etc.;
> (3) the results secured;
> (4) the means and the results considered in the relation of cause and effect.
>
> It is conceivable that in accomplishing this task the psychologist may encounter phenomena transcending what he can explain by the causes already known. So-called premonitions, clairvoyance, telepathy, sudden moral conversions, and mystic illuminations might, for instance, baffle his efforts at explanation. And it might be claimed that the course of historical events testifies to a divine action.
>
> These are possibilities; but let this be clearly seen: it is for science to show that any one of these possibilities has become at a particular time a reality. The facts must first be analyzed, compared, classified, and an effort made to trace them back to familiar causes. (Leuba, 1912, pp. 268-9).

This statement is manifestly useless as a guide to life, since nobody could reasonably contend that present knowledge of psychology - let alone that in Leuba's day – is sufficient to provide a framework except for limited parts of life. The statement is essentially a working hypothesis for the psychological study of religion. As such it is sound, subject to the proviso that the techniques available to the psychologist are sensitive enough to detect the "phenomena transcending what he can explain by the causes already known." We shall see in a later chapter that this proviso may be important.

Both Leuba and many religious people who have been disturbed by his views, have fallen into the error of assuming that analysis destroys what is analysed. This is not so: to describe religious conversion as a reorientation of the personality which is substantially conditioned by the social environment, does not destroy conversion or detract from its significance, any more than sugar ceases to exist, or no longer tastes sweet, when we know that it consists of carbon, hydrogen and oxygen. Nor is the value of a thing or event in one setting necessarily the same as in another. If, for example, some of the sexual impulses appearing in some religious experiences are of a kind that we should normally regard as perverted, this does not condemn the religious experience concerned any more than a quarryman is to be condemned for using dynamite because it can also be used by a burglar to blow a safe.

A second group of psychologists who have concerned themselves with religion is represented by Jung (1933, 1938), Adler (1938), Weatherhead (1929), Johnson (1953) and others. These authors have compared the practical effects of religion with those of psychotherapy pointing out, for example, the similarity between the psychotherapist's attempt to bring "integration" to the emotional life of a patient, and the focusing by religion of a man's powers on the service of God. From this they conclude that religion is, or can be, useful as a means of attaining or preserving mental health, and Jung goes so far as to adopt a great deal of Christian language in expressing his views although he does not always, as Thouless (1959) observes, use his words with their usual Christian meanings. This type of approach has been valuable in promoting co-operation between psychotherapists and clergy, giving the former a tool, and the latter a perspective, which they did not have before.

The results obtained by this group are often regarded as a justification of religion, but this claim is not valid. The studies on which it is based are too limited in scope, almost all being concerned with the application to neurotic behaviour of highly controversial theories which lie outside the main stream of normal scientific psychology. Any general treatment of religion needs to be made against a much broader psychological background. What is more, parallels between religious and psychological phenomena no more justify religion than they destroy it, and to use them as an argument for the truth or worth of religion is to commit the same kind of error as that made by the first group. The beneficial effects of religious activities on certain neurotic conditions might prove to have been due to some relatively trivial feature, such as the companionship gained from belonging to a church society, and be effective even if religious doctrines were false and church services unedifying.

These criticisms do not attach to the third group of psychologists who have looked at religion in psychological terms. Their attempt has been neither to condemn nor to justify, but to view religious experience and behaviour as a part of human activity, and thus as open to psychological study to the same extent and in the same way as any other part. Leading representatives of this group include Starbuck (1899), James (1902), Thouless (1923), Allport (1951) and Argyle (1958), and their books are worthwhile reading for every serious student of either religion or psychology. It is perhaps significant that all these authors have been known and respected for their broad grasp of general psychological issues. The knowledge they have contributed is as yet fragmentary, so that a reader looking for a coherent body of knowledge will be disappointed. Anyone, however, who has done research in a relatively unexplored field, will know that a long process of accumulating such fragments is usually necessary before they can be pieced together into any reliable larger structure.

THE WAY AHEAD

Looking back, we can see that the study of religion in psychological terms has been hampered, on the one hand, by the ignorance, fear and entrenched ideas of many religious people and, on the other hand, by the arrogant simple-mindedness of many psychologists who have reflected the attitudes typical of scientists around the turn of the century. In the main, however, progress has been slow because the theories and concepts of psychology have not been ready to tackle phenomena as complex as religion. Modern experimental and social psychologists are just beginning to develop their techniques for studying, and their theories for understanding, human behaviour in its full complexity. The aim of this book is to look at some aspects of religion in terms of these developing ideas, trying not so much to achieve a comprehensive, coherent view, as to illustrate a way of looking at particular problems of religious belief and practice.

Although the psychological study of religion has been going on now for some seventy years, it is still in its infancy, and we may well ask what we can expect of it when it reaches maturity. Undoubtedly the most fundamental achievement should be a clearer insight into the way in which religious behaviour and experience are related to human needs and capacities, looking beyond conscious thoughts and feelings to include also the many rational and irrational processes of brain and mind of which we are scarcely, if at all, aware. Such insight should include a better understanding than we have at present of the functions of religion both in normal daily life and in various special circumstances, the way in which religion develops during childhood through adolescence and adulthood to old age, the factors which engender or destroy religious belief, the roots of different types of religious attitude, and the human and social factors which make the various churches the kind of societies they are. Such new knowledge is not likely to bring about a revolution of ideas which would mean the end of religion as we now know it: just as the application of scientific knowledge to a traditional industry tends often to refine and develop what has been done hitherto rather than sweep it away, so in the case of religion we should expect clarifications and changes of emphasis rather than the complete overthrow of old ideas. In particular, we might hope for the translation into a more readily understood idiom of terms such as *grace, sin, revelation, righteousness, sacrifice, faith, justification* and even *prayer* and *love*. These terms have over the years gradually become a technical jargon, which is as much a barrier to understanding of the Christian message as the technical jargon of science is to popular appreciation of scientific attainments and potential contributions.

We cannot look to psychological studies for proof of the ultimate value of religion, since this involves questions of the purpose of life and of the universe which are beyond the scope of science. We can, however, look for judgements of value at a more elementary level. We have already noted the effectiveness of religion as an aid in the treatment of some neuroses. It should be possible to gain a much clearer idea than we have at present, of the extent to which particular religious activities help in dealing with the demands of life, and aid particular types of person. Looking at the problem from another angle, it should be possible to assess the likely consequences of particular religious beliefs and practices, and so to assign priorities and match activities to circumstances.

It is sometimes argued that religion has retreated as science has advanced. For example, biblical doctrines about the creation of the world and of man have yielded to the discoveries made by geology and biology, and religious concepts of disease have given way before the advances of medicine and biochemistry. Evidence cited in favour of such views is not only the decline in church attendance which has coincided with the spread of scientific knowledge, but the loss of religious faith by individuals as they become more knowledgeable. Both lines of evidence are, however, questionable. The movement away from the churches seems more likely to have been due to their having failed to incorporate developing ideas into their thinking, and also to economic changes which have made it difficult for independent bodies burdened with the increasingly heavy cost of maintaining property, to keep up their service to the community. In any case, the move away from religion has been far from continuous: for instance in the U.S.A., Gilliland (1953) found a substantial and fairly continuous rise of favourable attitudes to religion among students from 1933 to 1949, and Bender (1958) found a similar rise from 1946 to 1956.

As regards individuals, it is true that several studies have shown that students tend progressively to become less favourable to religion and more critical of religious beliefs as they go through the later years of school and university (e.g. Brown & Lowe, 1951, Gilliland, 1953, Poppleton & Pilkington, 1963, Havens, 1964, Hites, 1965), but these changes seem to be due at least in part to social influences and to the rebelliousness of youth against the beliefs inculcated in childhood. The changes observed seem to reflect the norms of the school or college concerned: on the one hand, Mull (1947) noted that the usual trend did not occur in a college with a strong religious tradition, and on the other hand Wright & Cox (1967a) found the decline of religion to be greater among girls at co-educational schools than at girls' schools, due seemingly to greater contact with boys whose religious attitudes are on average less favourable than those of girls. Once school and college days are over, attitudes seem to become more favourable to religion (Bender, 1958).

Looking at the evidence in more detail, the signs of turning away from religion have been mainly in the decline of church attendance and of scores on certain questionnaires. These have taken as their measure of favourableness to religion, the willingness to endorse a number of somewhat crude ideas about the nature of God, the literal truth of the Bible and disapproval of birth control. These ideas are indeed intellectually weak, and it is perhaps not surprising that those who hold them have been found, on average, to score substantially less on intelligence tests than those who are critical of them (Brown & Lowe, 1951). The main evidence in favour of an increase of religious feeling has come from other questionnaires which have examined more positive religious attitudes towards the world and fellow men. It is in line with this that, among university students who retain their religion, there seems to be a move away from small sects towards larger churches (Garrison, 1962), and from crudely anthropomorphic, pictorial ideas of God to more abstract, spiritual concepts (McCann, 1959).

The tendencies among adolescents can be seen as the continuation of trends among children. A number of studies have shown that as children grow older, especially between about fourteen and seventeen years of age, their belief that prayer can affect external events, such as the weather, declines, and that magical and animistic concepts of prayer give way to ideas of praying with a view to modifying one's own attitudes (Jahoda,

1958, Godin & van Roey, 1959, Thouless & Brown, 1964, Brown, 1966, 1968). The trends are independent of denomination and have been found in several different countries, including Belgium, Australia, Ghana, New Zealand and the United States. They are, perhaps, part of a general decline in religious dogmatism (Anderson, 1962), self-centredness (Ugurel-Semin, 1952) and suggestibility (McConnell, 1963) in children as they acquire more contact with others, and attain better structured ideas about the world.

Taking all the evidence together, it seems fair to suggest, that what has been regarded as a turning away from religion as knowledge advances is, for both society and individuals, to be construed rather as a swing away from myth, superstition, unreasoned authoritative pronouncements, prejudice and purely formal religious observance, to a more informed set of beliefs. These are often at variance with the religious teaching given by some denominations, but are sincere and based on values which have been accepted freely after careful thought.

Chapter II

What is Religion?

WE CAN all say with fair confidence that a particular act, object, principle or idea is religious while another is not, yet most of us would be at a loss to define religion if we were challenged to do so. Such inability is found in other situations as well. The skilled tradesman in a factory often has very little idea of how he does his job, and if he tries to put his techniques into words, he is likely to be only partly correct in what he says. The same is true of experts in many games such as cricket, football, tennis or golf. At a less concrete level, the assessment of intelligence is now an established part of educational procedure in many developed countries, yet nobody has a really clear idea of what intelligence is, or of what is being measured by intelligence tests.

It is thus understandable that none of the many attempts that have been made to define religion seems wholly convincing. Leuba (1912) collected forty-eight definitions current in the early years of the present century, and many have since swelled the list. They vary widely because religion has been of interest to many branches of philosophical, social and psychological study, and each has viewed it from its own standpoint. For our present purposes, definitions divide essentially into two groups: first, those which seek to identify some unique feature of experience or behaviour which can be regarded as a hallmark of religion; and second, those which try to discover its origin or purpose. We shall look at both these groups before attempting a definition on rather different lines.

THE SEARCH FOR DISTINCTIVE FEATURES

The attempt to identify particular psychological processes by which to define religion, was especially characteristic of the late nineteenth century. Three types of definition were explored: intellectual, emotional and behavioural. We shall consider these types in turn.

Intellectual formulae

Several authors saw the essence of religion as a process of reasoning, and therefore sought to define it in terms of concepts, understanding or knowledge: man finds himself confronted by a mysterious universe, of which he demands an explanation. An important part of almost every religion is indeed an account of how a deity or deities created the world, and have since maintained the world order. The account sets man in his place in nature, and portrays the main outlines of the superhuman power or powers with which he has to deal. The details are embodied not only in what are essentially mythologies, such as the Greek and Roman legends and the stories in the early books of the Bible, but also in official creeds and doctrines to which adherents are expected to subscribe. These latter may be regarded by many as irksome quibbles, but they appear to be especially likely to enter as a religion develops. For example, Thouless (1940) notes that Buddhism originally had as one of its guiding principles, the belief that doctrines and speculations must be avoided. Within a comparatively short time, however, it came to be equipped with just the formulations its founder had condemned.

Once established, doctrines and creeds do in a very real sense define the religion concerned, and tend to be tenaciously preserved. For instance, in present-day Christianity there is a fair willingness to accept fresh ideas about the interpretation of the Bible, revised forms of church service and new methods of church government, but any attempt to change doctrine meets with stiff resistance.

The particular formulae that define various religions and denominations differ substantially, and it seems impossible to single out any one feature which is characteristic of religion as such, and able to distinguish it from other systems of beliefs and ideals, such as those of some professional bodies, or of movements such as the Scouts, or of political faiths such as communism. Even more, we cannot point to a body of knowledge, or manner of gaining it, which is especially religious as opposed to, say, scientific: there seems to be no single formula which is necessary and sufficient as a specification of religion. For our fundamental definition we must, therefore, look elsewhere.

Emotions and feelings

For many people, religion is not a matter of intellect but of emotions and feelings. Conversely, religious behaviour tends to arise in situations of great emotional stress — people tend to pray in danger and to give thanks to God in times of great joy.

Those whose religion is mainly a matter of feeling, resemble those with a more intellectual approach in sensing a mystery in the universe, but unlike them, they are content to leave the mystery unsolved. Some of them report what they regard as moments of great insight, but these seem not to be due to the precipitation of knowledge, so much as to taking a fresh look at the mystery. One may question the nature and validity of at least some of these insights. Feelings are often deliberately cultivated in primitive religious practices by the use of incantations, suggestion and even drugs, such as peyote which contains the hallucination-producing substance mescalin. The effect of such practices and drugs seems to be to divorce the experience of the moment from the context of other events, in terms of which it is normally perceived. For example, the colours we see in ordinary circumstances are determined not only by the actual wavelengths of light reflected by objects, but by the relations between these and the wavelengths and intensities of the light reflected by surrounding objects. The reader can verify this for himself by looking through a narrow tube, first at a piece of grey paper near a window, and then at a piece of white paper in deep shadow. If he looks at the papers in such a way that he sees nothing of their surrounding objects, the white paper in shadow will look *darker* than the grey paper in good light. In short, the perceived whiteness of objects depends on the relationship between the light reflected by them and by surrounding objects – the lightest object in any given area of illumination appears white, and other objects are scaled accordingly. Drugs such as mescalin seem to prevent these relationships exerting an effect, with the result that colours may appear unusual and often surprisingly intense. The same seems to be true of other relationships between objects and their surroundings in space and time, so that ordinary objects may appear intensely beautiful or threatening or important (Huxley, 1954). Similar effects, although usually on a lesser scale, can be produced by means of suggestion, hypnosis and other methods of restricting the context of attention.

Emotions in face of the more striking phenomena of nature, such as storms, thunder, floods and eclipses, have been prominent in primitive religions. Emotions still play an important part in developed, present-day religion, including both fear, as in certain types of evangelical preaching, and feelings of a more aesthetic nature in music, art and the literature of liturgy, as we shall see further in Chapter 5. The latter feelings often go with a religious tradition which, intellectually, is highly sophisticated. All these emotions and feelings seem, however, to have their counterparts in experiences which would not normally be regarded as religious. Thus, for example, any unresolved mystery can cause fear if it implies a possible threat, any powerful object may be awe-inspiring whether or not we endow it with divine attributes, and any research scientist knows that a new insight can bring elation and feelings of intense pleasure (c.f. Watson, 1968).

Codes of Behaviour

Every religion seems to involve behaviour by prescribing a system of ethics and a set of rituals. Both seem to be essential: even the determined lack of ceremony by Quakers must be regarded as a kind of ceremonial. The prescribed behaviour includes both individual acts such as private devotions, and also communal acts such as ritual gatherings or church services. The former seem usually to be shaped by norms learnt from public religious activities, and thus to reflect the religious and social background in which the individual was brought up. The latter are commonly symbolic of the mythology and doctrine of the religion or denomination concerned, although they are not entirely bound to it. On the one hand, ritual may change whereas doctrines do not, as in the revised services which have recently come into use in the Church of England and the Roman Catholic Church. On the other hand, rituals may continue but their meanings may change, as with the many pagan feasts and ceremonies which have been taken over and given new meaning in Judaism and Christianity.

Like doctrines, rituals and ceremonies vary with religion and denomination to such an extent that it is impossible to point to particular acts which are diagnostic of religion as a whole. Much the same can be said of ethical principles. Furthermore, there is a substantial overlap between religious ethics and those which are avowedly non-religious. For example, however wide apart Christianity may be from humanism and communism, many principles such as those of faithful, honest dealing, sinking ones own desires in the welfare of the larger community, and caring about one's fellow men, are common to them all. It may be argued that this is understandable, since the non-religious ideas concerned have grown up within a culture firmly rooted in centuries of Christianity, but it does mean that such principles are no longer the exclusive marks of Christianity. Indeed it takes little knowledge of history to realise that they never were.

To sum up our discussion so far, we can say that although intellectual formulations, emotions and actions are all involved in religion, we are not able to pick out any one formula, feeling or act which we can point to as the essential of religion. Something more subtle and complex, if less tangible and less readily identified, seems to be required.

ORIGINS AND USES

Many of the different views which have been put forward to account for the origins of religion, reflect the nature-nurture conflict, which has run through many other areas of psychological theory ever since the subject became a separate field of study. How far does religion arise as the result of inherited tendencies, and how far as a result of experience and training?

The first view is represented by several writers who have claimed that religion is an instinct, and thus belongs to the basic nature of man. The description is plausible, in that religion is one of the most universal of cultural phenomena in both primitive and advanced civilisations. Also, it seems to be readily adopted by children – it comes "naturally" to them.

The biological use of the term "instinct" is to define behaviour which comes into being as an animal develops, without any process of learning. The most clear-cut examples of this occur in insects, some of which show quite complex patterns of behaviour that are carried out perfectly without having been learnt. In mammals, including man, instinctive behaviour is of less fixed form, and instincts are to be defined more in terms of inherited tendencies to seek certain goals which satisfy needs, such as for food and water, that are essential to the individual; or for sexual intercourse and the nurturing of young, without which the race would not survive. The detailed routines used to satisfy these needs are largely learnt: it is the needs themselves which derive from inherited biological constitution.

Evidence regarding the effects of experience on religion is not easy to interpret. Obviously the details of the ritual of any religion or denomination are learnt, usually in childhood: but what of the underlying tendency? Several studies have shown that an individual's religion usually resembles that of his parents and friends (see Argyle, 1958). Parents are an obvious source of teaching about details of religion, but how far acceptance or rejection is due to their training and how far to similarity of genetic make-up between parents and children, we do not know. As regards friends, we may in the same way ask whether similarity of religion results from mutual influence, or from the tendency to form friendships with those of like temperament? The same kind of question attaches to the religious awakenings that occur at evangelistic meetings, or in times of special stress, such as in battle, or at the loss of someone who has been very close. Such incidents undoubtedly precipitate religious activity in many people, but are they sufficient causes on their own, or are they effective only when the underlying personality is appropriate? The fact that not everyone who experiences these incidents reacts to them in a religious way, suggests that the latter is nearer the truth.

Seeming evidence that learning and experience play at least some part, comes from the tendency for children's religion to resemble that of their mothers more closely than that of their fathers (Newcomb & Svehla, 1937; Bell, 1938), and also from the effects, noted in the previous chapter, of college and school norms upon changes of religion during adolescence (Mull, 1947; Wright & Cox, 1967b). However, whether these factors are sufficient causes or whether they merely bring out latent, genetically based potentialities, and whether they affect basic religious tendency or merely the details of religious expression, is again open to question.

The varieties of religious behaviour are such that religion clearly is not an instinct in the sense of a fixed, inherited pattern of behaviour. It is, however, much more reasonable to suppose that there are in man's inherited constitution, features which lead him to view and react to particular events in life in ways we call religious. If so, there is a sense in which we can regard religion as instinctive. Doing so does not, however, get us very far: it merely leads to the further question of what are the particular events and ways of reacting to them, in which these inherited tendencies come into play? Putting the question another way, what function does religion have in life?

Psychoanalytic views on religion

Probably the best known writer who has attempted to answer this question is Freud. His early ideas on the origins of totem and taboo in primitive religion (Freud, 1919) make curiously tortuous and dated reading, which need not concern us here: they have been well discussed by Philp (1956). More significant

34

are his views on developed religion. He lays stress on man's helplessness in the face of cruel, hard fate, and on his struggle against the constraints that life in human society places upon him. Religion offers a means of escape from the rigours of the world and the bonds of society. It has a threefold function: to explain the origin of the universe, to give assurance of protection in life and of final happiness in spite of present hardships, and to provide an authoritative discipline. It thus satisfies man's desire for knowledge, for happiness and safety, and for benign guidance amid the turmoils and trials of life (Freud, 1928, 1933).

The key to the understanding of the way in which religion does this is contained in the view that God is a *substitute, ideal father*. Freud traces the development of the child who, in his childhood helplessness, receives protection from his father whom he regards as all-powerful. As the child grows to adulthood, he begins to realise that his father's powers are limited, and at the same time the world impinges more strongly and more cruelly upon him. In response to this situation the man "looks back to the memory-image of the overrated father of his childhood, exalts it into a Deity, and brings it into the present and into reality." (Freud, 1933, p.223).

Just as the child's father was the source of knowledge, so is man's god. As the child ran to its father for protection, so man looks to god. As the father disciplined the child, so god is regarded as the embodiment of authority and moral law.

This moral law, Freud maintains, derives from the disciplines of childhood incorporated by the man into his "super-ego". Because of this, the moral law can lead to serious personality difficulties. Childhood rules do not at all points apply well to adult life, and have to be revised. However, such revision involves a breach of the childhood discipline, and this breach, because it is with something incorporated very early into the individual's make-up, leads to feelings of *guilt*.

Freud suggests that the attempt to get rid of guilt feelings leads to obsessional or compulsion neurosis. In this state there is a tendency towards the performance of compulsive rituals such as continual hand-washing, the eating or avoidance of certain foods, or the arranging of furniture, house ornaments or clothes in particular ways. Freud points out that many religions use very similar rituals in the attempt to relieve feelings of guilt. Religion is thus conceived as a neurotic phenomenon. It represents, however, a kind of community neurosis which Freud believes can help worshippers to a state in which they are less likely to develop individual neurotic symptoms.

Freud's breakaway pupil Jung held views which were in many ways similar. To him, the major problem of life was the struggle that every child has to make, away from dependence on its mother, towards the ability to deal normally and independently with the realities of the world. This struggle is a severe one, and involves the renunciation and sacrifice by the adolescent of the care, peace, comfort and freedom from responsibility that were given it by its mother. It also involves shifting sexual energies away from the mother – or in the case of a girl from the father – to a new object round which the powers and energies of the individual can be concentrated, and by which they can be organised.

The normal goal of these instinctive energies is a mate of the opposite sex. For one reason or another, however, the normal goal may not be found. If this happens, one of two things may follow: there may either be regression, a return to fixation upon the mother; or the energy may be turned towards some other than normal object, in which case "sublimation" is said to occur. Religion is regarded by Jung as a focus of such sublimation. The conflict produced by the failure of the energies to find a normal object is projected onto another object, which then becomes symbolic of the struggles of the conflict. Thus in

Christianity, Jung regards the Crucifixion and Resurrection as symbolising the renunciation of the mother's care that is necessary for the attainment of full adulthood (Jung, 1938).

Jung regarded religion as a valuable means of helping his neurotic patients to adjust themselves to life. He held that it not only provided an adequate counter to any tendency to regress towards childish dependence, but also incorporated many of the features which make regression attractive to the neurotic. He says:

The benefits of religion are the benefits of parental hands; its protection and its peace are the results of parental care upon the child; its mystic feelings are the unconscious memories of the tender emotions of the first childhood. (Jung, 1933, p. 99).

To Freud's other well-known breakaway pupil, Adler, the key to the maze of life's intricacies lies in man's upward struggle towards betterment and perfection, in realisation of his own weakness, and in desire for mastery. Adler suggests that the feeling of being inferior in any particular, leads to striving in order to compensate for the inferiority and turn it into superiority. Thus, just as a man who is blind usually uses his hearing very much more effectively than sighted people, so a man who is physically weak often develops a degree of moral courage and persuasiveness which, in his dealings with others, more than makes up for his physical disability.

If man's strivings after superiority do not find some socially constructive goal, they will find a less desirable one, such as crime, imaginary illness, or excessive criticism as a means of gaining control over other people and so becoming superior to them.

Of the various goals worth striving for, Adler lists religion as one, and he regards it as important and valuable. He says:

The best conception hitherto gained for the elevation of humanity is the idea of God. There can be no question that the idea of God really includes within it as a goal the movement towards perfection, and that as a concrete goal, it best corresponds to the obscure yearnings of human beings to reach perfection. There are no doubt conceptions of God that from the very start fall far short of the principle of perfection; but of its purest form we can say—here the presentation of the goal of perfection has been successful. (Adler, 1938, pp. 272–3).

The method of attaining the goal is still that of imaginative thought: Adler postulates that the idea of perfection, coupled with knowledge of inferiority, produces a number of desires that man realises can never be fulfilled. In particular, he speaks of man's desire to be the omnipotent master of the world, and this Adler sees as producing ideas of an omnipotent-miracle-working god.

Religion as a search for control

A view of religion which is in many ways similar to that of Jung and Adler, but based on what is known of normal perception and thinking, has been set out by Flower (1927) and by Bartlett (1950), under whom Flower worked at Cambridge. Their approach begins from the fact that if any object is seen, or event occurs, the processes of recognising it and giving it meaning involve a more or less elaborate process of searching the memory, constructing hypotheses, and testing them before final acceptance. In normal life, these processes usually occur so quickly that we do not observe them: perception and meaning come so easily, we do not analyse the way in which they are attained. Sometimes, however, the process is more difficult and protracted. When, for example, we look at a puzzle picture of the kind that shows a familiar object from an unusual angle, we may at first be unable to name it. If so, we examine it carefully and try to think of some object it might be, probably running through several and rejecting them. We may then think of objects and imagine them turned to unusual angles, and so on until a solution is found. The solution may not be complete — we may, for instance, say that the object is *like* something but not the same.

Similar processes occur in the face of unusual situations: we may not know how to cope with them, but the desire or necessity of doing something about them remains. In such cases, we resort to imaginative thinking. If this produces an appropriate plan of action, the situation is brought under control and we say that our thinking has been "rational" and "normal". If, however, the situation remains mysterious and baffling, we cannot deal with it completely. It is then, Flower suggests, that we may make a religious response as representing a possible means of bringing the situation under some sort of control. In other words, Flower proposes that religion functions to provide a means of responding to what he calls a "beyond" element in our experience.

Bartlett says what is, in effect, much the same when he emphasises that effective action demands that we go beyond present evidence, extrapolating to future events, and making intuitive judgements when no certain knowledge exists. In short, belief and acting on faith are inevitable, and religion is a systematic set of beliefs.

In both Flower's and Bartlett's views, religion is thus a form of thinking which differs from what we call normal, rational thought in that its propositions are inevitably less open to direct verification. It may nevertheless be important as a means of making sense of the world, and as providing a basis for coherent action.

Frustration and religion

Running through all the views on the origins of religion that we have outlined, is the essential theme that religion is, in some way, a means of dealing with the frustrations of life by making use of an imaginatively constructed world. Here we have a hypothesis that is open to scientific test.

Some indication that the hypothesis is correct is contained in the finding that psychotic patients suffering from religious delusions had histories of frustrated social and emotional needs, due to poverty or to social or marital difficulties (Lowe, 1954).

Argyle (1958) has collected sociological evidence which suggests that those sections of the community which suffer the greatest frustration do indeed tend to be more religious than some others: for instance in 1946 the number of American negroes who were church members was seventy-one, against fifty-five for white people. Membership of minor protestant sects of the ecstatic "hell-fire" type in America, has tended to be among those who were very poor or of low social status. It has been argued that the beliefs of these sects are compensatory, making virtues of poverty, frugality and industry, and predicting an early end to the world, when the rich will be punished and the humble rewarded (Clark, 1937). Again, older people and those with chronic illness, perhaps fearing death, tend to be more religious than younger, fit people (e.g. Pan, 1952); and widows, who might be regarded as socially, sexually and often economically frustrated, have been found to be more religious than married women. Religious beliefs in these cases might again be compensatory, holding out hope for survival and reunion after death.

Sociological evidence in favour of religion being a response to frustration is not, however, entirely clear. For example, in America where the fullest statistics are available, church membership of white people in the 1940s and 1950s tended to be greater among the well-to-do than among the poor, and among the middle classes than among the lower. Christian beliefs in general can hardly be said to be compensatory for well-to-do middle class people. We can only speculate as to why church membership should rise with economic and social status in this way. The evidence regarding negroes and small sects seems to rule out the possibility that poor people do not have the time, energy or opportunity to go to church. One possible explanation is that middle-class and well-to-do people tend, on average, to be abler than others, and that able people tend to aim at higher standards of achievement, and to be more concerned with the possibility of failure, than those less gifted. If so, religion could still be for them a reaction to frustrations, but to ones which were imagined as potential dangers rather than actually present.

Evidence of a different kind comes from an experimental study in which subjects were given six short anecdotes and asked, in each case, whether or not they would pray in the circumstances described (Welford, 1947a,b). Three of the situations outlined were unpleasant or distressing, and three pleasant. Many more subjects said they would pray in the former, although a substantial number said they would also pray in the latter.

Subjects were also asked to rank the six situations, first according to the extent that they would "stir their emotions"; second, according to the extent to which they would be unable to cope with the situations except by praying – in other words, according to the extent to which they would be frustrating; and third, according to how likely they would be to pray.

The results showed that frustration in this sense was an important factor leading to prayer, but not the only one. The likelihood of prayer rose with emotion as well as frustration. The correlations were such as to imply that the relationships of

41

prayer to both these variables were substantially independent, so that the relationship with emotion could not be accounted for by supposing that emotion results from frustration, or vice-versa. Individual subjects varied substantially, some indicating that prayer was, for them, more strongly associated with emotion, and others regarding it as more closely linked with frustration. The correlations held, not only for all six situations taken together, but also within the three unpleasant situations and the three pleasant ones separately. It may be wondered how pleasant situations can also be frustrating, but subjects regarded them as being so in the sense that they felt they would be unable to express their pleasure or joy adequately: prayer in these situations appeared to be concerned with gratitude and worship.

Apart from expressing gratitude, there have, historically, been two aims of prayer: first to control or coerce a deity or to secure his favour; and second to align oneself with divine will. Most people today would, if challenged, regard the first as absurd, at least as a means of influencing physical events – we no longer pray for rain or fine weather, despite the inclusion of prayers for each in the Church of England Prayer Book. Instead, we have shifted towards the second view of prayer. We can, however, see how the first view came to be held: if the deity is regarded as a kind of super-man, it is reasonable to address him humbly in the hope that he will change his mind about unpleasant events, or mete out favours. Such behaviour sometimes appears to be rewarded: fine weather goes in spells, so that if there has been a long drought which has brought people to the point of praying for rain, it is not unlikely that rain will follow within a few days. If it does, the prayer will seem to have been answered. Praying for rain in this way is not likely to be discouraged by failure of rain to follow on some occasions: several experiments have shown that behaviour which is only occasionally rewarded may, in fact, be more frequently repeated than behaviour which is rewarded consistently (see e.g. Kimble, 1961, pp. 160–4). Similar principles probably apply to many types of superstition: fortunate and unfortunate events, either important or trivial, occur every day, and in seeking to understand why they have occurred, it is easy to connect them with some event which has gone before. Sometimes the connection is in a sense justified: for example, spilling salt may imply that we are passing through a period during which our actions are being hurried and careless, so that we are indeed more liable to misfortune in the form of accidents. Once we have gained the idea that an event or action is "unlucky", its occurrence may make us anxious, and so again more liable to accident than we usually are.

To return to the results of our experiment, there were very few signs of prayer being regarded as a means of securing miraculous, divine intervention in the physical world. Nor was prayer regarded as a passive means of escape from the world and its rigours, or as an appeal to God as a father by someone feeling himself in the position of a child. Rather it was regarded as an active means of trying to deal with situations which were unusual or baffling, in which other responses had been tried and failed, or seemed useless. In short, prayer was for help in overcoming a problem or in adjusting oneself to it: it was a supplement to, rather than a substitute for, other action.

These results seem more in line with the views of Flower and Bartlett than with those of Freud, Jung and Adler. At least among our subjects, who were all actually or nominally Christians, religion was not a way of escape from cruel fate into the arms of a substitute parent, nor was it a means of sublimation or compensation. Instead, it was one among many techniques of grappling actively with the problems of life.

Effects of religion

From the relationship between prayer and emotion found in our experimental results, we might at first sight expect that more emotionally labile individuals would be more likely to pray. On the other hand, Freud makes the very reasonable suggestion that, if religion is doing its work well, it will tend to make people more stable emotionally than they would otherwise be (Freud, 1928, p. 77). Additional results of our experiment are in line with Freud's view. After completing their ratings of the situations, subjects filled in a personality questionnaire. Such questionnaires are crude instruments for assessing personality, but have been shown to give some useful rough indications. In the present case, scores indicating emotional stability tended to increase with the number of situations in which subjects said they would pray. The trend was, however, not very pronounced, and there was a great deal of variation between individuals. We should, perhaps, not be surprised at this. The subjects who were most stable emotionally, might tend *not* to pray because few events would move them sufficiently either to pray or to do anything else. Again, some of the least stable would be so disorganised that they could do nothing effective, either in the form of prayer or otherwise, whereas some would pray a great deal, finding that it helped, but was not enough to cure their condition. Any such cases would tend to obscure the overall trend for emotional stability to increase with religious observance. That such cases exist, is suggested by the finding that members of an extreme Protestant institution were more subject to nervous symptoms than the average person (Kimber, 1947), while a more representative group showed that religion tended to go with less tendency to pathological behaviour (Meadow & Bronson, 1969).

Further indications that religion has beneficial effects are that those who score highly on various tests of "religiosity", tend to have high standards of conduct and greater self-confidence (Brown & Lowe, 1951), greater feeling of security, and less anxiety and fear of death (Brown, 1962, Williams & Cole, 1968, Martin & Wrightsman, 1965). Also, those who respond to calls for religious dedication at revivalist meetings show less anxiety and stress when they have done so, than they did before (Cooley & Hutton, 1965). Those with a favourable attitude to the church have been found to use less tobacco, alcohol, tea and coffee, presumably being less dependent upon the solaces these provide (Telford, 1950). Again, well-adjusted old people tend to engage in more religious activities than their contemporaries, although in this case it is not clear whether the religious activities are the cause of the better adjustment, or vice versa (Moberg, 1956). It has also been noted that *Who's Who in America* and *American Men of Science* contain the names of an unduly high proportion of the sons and grandsons of clergy, ministers and missionaries (for a brief review see Clark, 1955).

On the other hand, high scores on certain tests of "religiosity" have been found to go with some tendencies that have been regarded as less satisfactory. Examples are dependence (Dreger, 1952), anti-semitic and anti-negro attitudes (e.g. Allport & Kramer, 1946; O'Reilly & O'Reilly, 1954; Blum & Mann, 1960), relatively low intelligence (see Argyle, 1958, p.93), and especially what has been termed "authoritarianism" (e.g. Adorno et al. 1950; Gregory, 1957; Jones, 1958; Brown, 1962). One study also failed to find any relationship between religious belief or behaviour, and humility of attitude or showing love and compassion for one's fellow men (Cline & Richards, 1965).

It must in fairness be said that these unfavourable indications can be questioned on four grounds. First, there are several different kinds of "religiosity": for example, "fundamentalist" as opposed to "humanitarian" (Broen, 1957); involving individual as opposed to group observance (Welford, 1959); and "extrinsic" as opposed to "intrinsic" (e.g. Allport, 1954; Jeeves, 1959; Allport & Ross, 1967). This last distinguishes a form of religion which is formal, institutionalised and *used* by its adherents, from one which is taken as a master guide to life and *lived* by its devotees. Studies have shown that the unfavourable attitudes which have been attributed to religious people, attach to the former type very much more than to the latter (e.g. Wilson, 1960).

Second, as already noted (p. 25), most of the studies have measured "religiosity" in terms of willingness to endorse a series of statements which reflect either fundamentalist Protestant positions such as the literal truth of the Bible, or rigid Roman Catholic dictates such as disapproval of artificial birth control. Few thinking religious people would score highly on these tests. They are, in effect, measures of an extreme type of religion likely to appeal only to uncritical and unimaginative people. It is therefore not surprising if those who endorse these statements about religion tend also to be unintelligent and hidebound in other departments of life. In line with this view, Martin and Nichols (1962) found that scores on a scale of religious belief rose with amount of religious knowledge among subjects whose knowledge was relatively poor, but fell with increased religious knowledge among those who were better informed. In other words, the really well informed cannot go along with the cruder religious beliefs.

Third, many of the questions on which assessments of so-called racial "prejudice" are based, take the form of general statements about Jews or negroes and do not make any provision for qualified answers. For example, the statement "The trouble with letting Jews into a nice neighbourhood is that they gradually give it a typical Jewish atmosphere" (Allport & Kramer, 1946, p. 12) can hardly be answered satisfactorily in terms of simple agreement or disagreement. Does it mean *any* Jewish family? Or an average Jewish family? Would the undesirable "atmosphere" be something produced only by Jews, or might it also follow if certain other groups, such as nurses or university professors, moved into the district? Nor is there usually opportunity to give reasons for answers, and without them, replies may be misleading. For instance, to endorse the statement "I should not wish to marry a Roman Catholic" might not imply, as it is usually assumed to do in America, feeling against the people of Irish or Italian origins who form the majority of the Roman Catholic community, but might only mean a wish not to have the large family that could result from refusal to practise birth control.

Fourth, we may question whether the so-called "authoritarian" personality is well named, or at any rate whether it deserves all the scorn that has been heaped upon it. The "authoritarian" has been regarded as an inflexible, unimaginative, intolerant, over-conforming, prejudiced disciplinarian. Yet, if one looks closely at the questionnaire statements used to define him, it seems fair to describe him also as a person who is prepared to sacrifice some spontaneity for stability, some permissiveness for the sake of order and peace, some immediate pleasure for the pursuit of long-term aims, and some sentimental toleration for the sake of efficiency. He may, of course, go too far in these directions, and may not appear as a gay, interesting person with whom immediate easy friendship is possible. A substantial measure of his qualities is, however, essential for dealing responsibly with the world as it is, and even more for making any worthwhile ideals come true.

RELIGION AS A COMPUTER PROGRAMME

Looking back over the various ideas about the origins and functions of religion that we have outlined, we again find that the identification of particular features essential to religion eludes us. Religion is a result of baffling situations, but it seems to be only one possible result among many. It offers a method of coping with these situations, but other methods are also possible. We cannot, therefore, define religion in terms of origins and functions, any more than we can in terms of formulae, emotions or activities.

The fundamental error behind most, perhaps all, of these attempts has been the belief that, basically, the human brain and nervous system act as a kind of telephone exchange, connecting sense organs to muscles, so that when a particular stimulus appears, an associated action occurs. The human sensory-motor system may act in this way for very simple reflexes, but the principle becomes extremely difficult to apply to more complex perception and action. How, for example, do we recognise an object such as a book, as the same when we see it from different angles? How do we perceive the room we are sitting in as "out there", and the objects in it as at different distances in space? The answer lies in the fact that normally our perception is not based on the momentary stimulations produced by simple objects. Rather, the brain seems automatically to perform a number of routine operations on incoming sense data, comparing one set with another, integrating over space and time, selecting and ordering. Thus, for example, the room we perceive around us is not at all like what is seen at any one glance – we have only to stare fixedly at one point to verify that this is so. Instead, it is a kind of composite picture, built up from many different glances, into which the fresh data from each new glance are incorporated.

Similar principles apply to action. Any movement, say of the hand, depends to some extent on the positions of almost every part of the body: the precise movement made grows out of the previous position of the hand, together with all the subtleties of posture at the time. There is thus a paradox in saying that we do the same thing twice. In one sense a repetition worker in industry carries out the same action over and over again, yet a detailed record of his performance would show that the precise course and timing of each action is slightly different from every other. The repeated action is thus an abstraction from a series of actions each of which is different from every other, in much the same way as the scene we perceive is an abstraction from the data provided by a series of different glances.

As we noted in the previous chapter, it is this kind of constancy in variety that is analogous to the operation of modern electronic computers. Essentially they deal with a *varied* mass of input data in terms of a *constant* programme, which relates individual items of input to other data, and produces a series of outputs. These could not be predicted from knowledge of either the input data or the programme alone, and would be different if either was changed.

It seems fair to argue that if there is anything uniquely diagnostic of religion in a psychological sense, it must lie in a programme of this kind. Once this is granted, several hitherto difficult questions receive relatively simple answers. Let us briefly look at four.

First, it becomes possible to define religion in terms of a pattern of ideas, emotions, actions, origins and functions, all of which individually are shared with other aspects of living: the pattern is unique only as a whole. The problem remains of whether any such unique pattern indeed exists, but the fact that people can conceive of "religion" as a recognisable entity even if they cannot define it, suggests that it does. The value of the computer analogy lies in its focusing the search for a definition of religion upon an area where there is reasonable hope of one being found.

Second, on the cognitive or "input" side, religion can be thought of as a set of rules, principles and procedures in terms of which input data are ordered or "coded", and events set in a framework of ideas and values, in terms of which they can be made to cohere and be given meaning. Such a framework will be subject to error and imperfections in that it is a structure of inferences – a "model" which is analogous to reality rather than reality itself. In this, however, religion is no different from most scientific theorising.

Third, on the action or "output" side, religion can be thought of as a set of principles for action which shape behaviour and deal with problems, in conformity with the ideas and values by which experience has been coded. Such a set of principles may produce action which varies according to circumstances, and changes as these change. This does not, however, imply that religious ethics and values are relative. It means that action which is true to certain constant underlying principles, *must* vary according to the details of the situation in which it occurs.

Lastly, religion will be, at one and the same time, a means of conservation and an agent of change. A constant programme means that recurrent situations – or to be precise *similar* situations – will be dealt with in similar ways, and provides a stable background behind the comings and goings, the ups and downs, of daily life and of shifting economic, social and political scenes. At the same time, it acts as a frame of reference which enables discrepancies between particular situations and optimum states to be recognised, thus providing a spur to action aimed at bringing about change.

Chapter III

The Concept of God

Man's ideas of deity have developed from a stage in which spirits inhabited springs and streams, trees and rocks, waves and storms; through the belief in many gods and goddesses dealing with different departments of life such as home, marriage, art or war, or of nature such as sun, moon, sea or crops; to the concept of one god supreme over all the universe. Progression on a smaller scale is seen also within the Old Testament, from a god of the Israelites who wars with the gods of surrounding nations, to one God who rules all the nations and can not only give Israel victory when she deserves it, but can bring in the Assyrians to punish Israel for her sins.

Such developing ideas are clearly within the field of modern psychological study; and recent research and thought on perception, which we have touched on in the previous chapter, suggest important ways of understanding how concepts of deity have arisen and progressed. Let us look at the processes of perception in rather more detail. At a relatively elementary level, incoming sense data are grouped and analysed in the brain so that, for example, lines, angles, coherent masses and groups of objects in close proximity are seen as wholes rather than as separate, discrete items. Thus we see a square as a single, unitary figure rather than as four separate lines which happen to join at the corners; and if we look at a face, we are aware of it as a whole before we observe the characteristics of the eyes, nose or mouth as separate features. As we noted before, such organisation extends over time as well as in space. We thus hear a series of notes as a single melody, or see a changing pattern of light and shade as a single object moving from one position to another.

Several studies made since about 1950 have emphasised that these principles of spatial and temporal integration are much more pervasive than is commonly recognised (Gibson, 1950, Welford, 1968, chapter 6). We have already pointed out that we do not normally perceive the pattern on the retina of the eye, but a "framework" built up from many different glances, which provides our stable "visual world", and into which the data from new glances are incorporated as they arrive. The framework provides a kind of running hypothesis about the world, which each new item of data either confirms or modifies. The "neural computer" in the brain seems to build this framework by detecting constants or "invariants" in the kaleidoscope of data coming in over space and time. It thus enables objects to be seen as such, although disturbed by random, interfering data: for instance a driver can see a car on the road ahead, even though his windscreen is covered by raindrops which obscure parts of the car's outline. In the same way, messages can be heard over a noisy telephone circuit, and one conversation can be picked out from others at a party.

The main lines of this organisation depend on mechanisms which are inherent in the brain, although they may require exercise to become fully functional: for example a man who is born blind and gains his sight in adulthood does not at first see objects clearly, although he does so after a few days (see Gregory, 1966). The details of organisation depend partly upon the pattern of past experience brought to the present situation, and partly upon the individual's hopes, fears, expectations and interests (Bartlett, 1932). Any present details which do not fit into these are either specially noted, or else are neglected – we all know how, if we meet a person unexpectedly, we either pick him out especially, or fail to observe him at all. At the same time, details which past experience or present desires might lead us to expect, may be "seen" even though they are not in fact present. The whole process seems to achieve an important *economy of effort* on the observer's part, in the sense that he deals with a few large, co-ordinated units of data, and can thus act more quickly than he could if he had to make decisions about a multiplicity of small items separately. Broadly speaking, perception seems to operate so as to account for the maximum amount of incoming sense data in the minimum number of perceptual — or more accurately *conceptual* — "units". This minimum number depends, to some extent, upon the precision required by the situation. Thus, for example, when waiting for a bus, all cars can be lumped together into one category, whereas if we are waiting for a friend to pick us up, different cars have to be distinguished. More generally, we can say that conceptual units or categories are such as to render the world more comprehensible, and thus more easily dealt with. Increased knowledge and sophistication leads, on the one hand, to the formation of larger more embracing units which enable general principles to be recognised; and on the other hand, to smaller units which permit more precise differences to be distinguished when necessary.

Categories or units dealing with concrete, static objects, seem always to have been easier to comprehend and define than those dealing with processes or activities. For example, the engine and body dimensions of a car are more readily understood than figures for performance; it is easier to rate schools in terms of buildings and equipment than on the quality of their teaching; and it seems easier to believe medical accounts attributing disease to bacteria viruses, or external agents such as carcinogens, than explanations in terms of stress or functional disturbance. If religion is a response to what Flower called a "beyond" element in experience, it is, therefore, not surprising that primitive religions developed deities in relation to things which were difficult to conceive in other ways. Primitive deities tended thus to be concerned with natural phenomena involving *activity*, such as heavenly bodies, streams and springs, wind and weather and were regarded as good or evil according to whether these were beneficent or hostile. Since these natural phenomena are complex and, at least to primitive man, somewhat unpredictable in their behaviour, it is understandable also that he should have thought of them in terms of the most familiar, complex, unpredictable objects in his experience, namely human beings or animals, and so given his deities human or animal form. We are, in many ways, less far removed from this stage of thinking than we realise: objects such as boats, ships or railway engines, the complexity of whose behaviour is not fully understood by those who are not experts, are often referred to as "she", and many of those who deal with complex electronic equipment describe it as "temperamental" when it shows an obscure, intermittent fault. We half-believe that these things have wills of their own, even though we know well that they have not (Brown & Thouless, 1965).

In moderately developed religions, such as those of ancient Greece, the seemingly chaotic interaction of various natural processes is explained by assuming that various deities compete and fight with each other. As insight into natural processes grows, it becomes possible to abstract more general principles, and thus to recognise that the chaos is not so chaotic after all. When this happens, religion seems first to postulate a hierarchical ordering among the gods, with some wielding power over the others; and finally arrives at the concept of one supreme god who rules over the whole of nature.

The abstraction involved in the idea of one supreme god

seems to have been difficult to attain. Abstract thinking of any sort is relatively difficult: it declines markedly in senility and in several forms of mental disease, and is less than normal in most mental defectives. The idea of a single supreme god thus tends to come at a late and sophisticated stage of human thinking, and even when it has been attained, the remains of earlier stages of thinking often remain. For example, the veneration of patron saints, in some Christian denominations, often comes close to the worship of local spirits in pagan times. Similar, perhaps, are the lingering beliefs in fairies among some country folk, and the half-beliefs in "gremlins" causing things to go wrong, which appeared among some aircrew under stress in the Second World War.

The Christian idea of God

To sum up our argument so far, the idea of deity seems to be a conceptual unit which ties together a range of experience, and which results in constants being detected behind the confusion of certain moment-to-moment events. This process makes it possible both to understand these events, and to respond to them effectively. The conceptual unit varies in size from relatively small, as in the case of primitive deities of trees or streams, through to an all-embracing unit covering the whole of reality, as in the case of God as understood by Christians. Thus conceived, God has essentially the same kind of status as physical concepts such as energy, electricity, or gravity. None of these can be directly observed: the proof of their existence lies in the extent to which they tie together facts which would not otherwise cohere. In the same way, proof of the existence of God must lie in the concept of God being better able than alternative concepts to rationalise a wide range of facts. Thinking of God in human terms is thus not strictly necessary, and may sometimes be misleading: for example a child's idea of God may be seriously distorted if, as often happens, he thinks of God as like his own father (Harms, 1944). It may, therefore, occasionally be necessary to abandon the human analogy in order to get an adequate comprehension of what is meant by God. For most people at most times, however, it is probably good enough, and often by far the best that is possible.

The approach we have outlined, accounts well for the main attributes normally ascribed to God by Christians. In cosmic terms, God can be described as *creator* of the world and universe because he personifies basic, ultimate reality. By the same tokens God is *omnipotent*. It is true that if man acts in a way which does not conform to basic reality, he is in a sense frustrating God, and thus rendering him seemingly not omnipotent; but the difficulty is resolved if the time-scale of action is taken into account. Man seems indeed liable to make choices which run counter to reality, yet at the same time he desires to understand and act on his understanding: this being so, reality must win in the end. On the more human side, God is *just* in the sense that flying in the face of reality brings unsatisfactory results. God is, however, *merciful* in that such results are not always catastrophic, and *forgiving* in that errors can be redeemed or made the basis of lessons for the future. Most important, God is *loving* in that human constitution is part of basic reality, so that fundamentally the natural world is supportive materially, and other people are supportive emotionally.

The view put forward here has inevitably been drawn in broad outline, and many objections to it will be advanced. Some of these may lose their force in the more detailed discussions of later chapters, but two need to be dealt with at once. First, it will be objected that God as envisaged here is a creation of human thought, instead of vice versa. In one sense this is true, but it must be remembered that conceptual frameworks built by different individuals seem to have substantial similarities, which suggest that they are all based on some common underlying reality, despite varying individual viewpoints. More important, conceptualisation and comprehension are not wholly the result of individual effort: they depend in part on inherited constitution, and very greatly on experience and training. These in turn depend on the experience and insights of those who have gone before us. In other words, our comprehension of the world, our awareness of what to look for in it, and understanding of how to deal with it, depend not so much on ourselves as on the circumstances in which we are born and brought up, on the precise circumstances and opportunities of our present material and human environment, and on the knowledge and cultural tradition handed down to us by previous generations. They are, in other words, the product of the larger reality around us as well as of our own brains. If so, then all conceptualisations, including our concept of God, are just as much — perhaps more — a revelation by God to us, as they are a discovery by us of God. Revelation and discovery are, in short, two facets of the same process.

The second objection we shall consider here, is that our concept of God is relative to present knowledge, and thus lacks stability. This also is in a sense true, but it is unfair to regard the fact as a criticism. We noted at the beginning of the chapter that the concept of God has developed greatly, even in biblical times. It can be reasonably argued that ideas of the nature of God have grown along with knowledge of the world and universe, following insights gained from grappling with the ever new problems besetting man at different times and places. For example, growth of the idea that God is Lord of the whole earth, was probably accelerated by the problem of rationalising the sufferings of the Israelites when defeated in war, and especially of good men oppressed by ruthless invaders. Despite such growth, and the changes it has brought, the concept of God has nevertheless remained stable in the sense that it has, at all stages, represented man's understanding of basic reality, according to the best that he knew at the time. The results of man's search, and of the revelations made to him, have all along been short of completeness, and when new insight has come, there has often been a change of emphasis. Yet the ultimate aim has always been the same, and development, when it has come, has been more the filling out of a picture and perceiving of its broader outlines, than the substituting of something wholly new for what was there before. This is all we can really ask. The incompleteness of knowledge admittedly means some lack of certainty, but the same is true of scientific theories, and the test that any proposed amendment must pass is the same both for these and for ideas about God: any new theory must incorporate facts that previous theories did not, while continuing to account for all the facts on which previous theories have been built.

A concept of God in these terms will doubtless be strange to many Christians and repugnant to some, yet it seems fair to claim that it is essentially in line with the ideas propounded in the opening verse of St. John's Gospel: "In the beginning was the Word, and the Word was with God, and the Word was God." Or, as it is translated in the New English Bible, "When all things began, the Word already was. The Word dwelt with God, and what God was, the Word was." The Greek *Logos* translated as "Word" also meant "reason" or "rationality" and seems further to have been used to denote what we should now call "basic reality" or "natural law". It would thus appear appropriate to translate:

In the beginning there was a basic, rational, natural law, and this natural law pertained to God—indeed it was God. Everything was created through this natural law—nothing was created outside it. All creation was enlivened by this law, including man to whom it gave the light of joy and deliverance—a light which shines in dark times and has never been quenched.

Such a translation makes better sense than either of the others, of what follows in the Gospel, and is probably closer to what the author of the Gospel would have said, had he been writing today.

ASPECTS OF GOD AND MAN

Let us now look a little more closely at the way the concept of God that we have outlined applies to traditional Christian interpretations of the world. Until comparatively recent times most Christian people seem to have divided their experience somewhat as follows:

1. *The Non-Human Environment*

    A. Objects which are either static or highly predictable in their behaviour. These have been regarded as constituting the "material world".

    B. Unpredictable processes and events. These have tended to be regarded as the works of God as the creator and manipulator of the universe—the term "act of God" is still used as a technical term in insurance policies to denote unpredictable natural events. In terms of the Christian concept of the Trinity, these activities seem to have been tacitly regarded as those of God in the person of the Father.

2. *Human Beings*

    A. Neutral actions: that is individual activities which have to do with the normal routine of everyday life, and which are regarded as neither especially good nor especially bad in either their intention or their outcome. These seem to have been taken as essentially human activity.

B. Good actions: that is actions, or patient refraining from action, which are especially constructive or beneficial in intention and outcome. These seem to have been typically regarded as due to divine promptings. In terms of the Trinity, they represented activity of the Holy Spirit.

C. Bad actions: that is actions, or failures to act, which are especially destructive or undesirable in either intention or outcome. These were attributed partly to social pressures, partly to individual weakness, and partly to personified evil —the "world, flesh and Devil" of the Church of England Prayer Book. The Devil was thought of as being able to affect intentions by disturbing human thought, and the outcome of human actions by manipulating the environment.

The view that both good and bad actions could be affected by invisible, non-material, external agencies was made the more plausible by the belief that everything essentially human in man's thoughts was open to introspection: many actions done under stress of emotion or resulting from unconscious motives, seem to be impelled from "outside", and thus to be due to some external agent.

Many people still divide their experience roughly in this way, although for most there have been two important changes. The first is that the distinction between predictable and unpredictable non-human events (i.e. 1 A and B) has largely broken down. A great deal of what was formerly unpredictable has become predictable as a result of advances in scientific knowledge and the spread of thinking in statistical terms. At the same time, even the most apparently stable objects have been shown to be not wholly predictable, at least on a sub-microscopic scale. To some people, these changes have made the concept of God redundant. To others, they have emphasised the idea of God as a unifying force behind material things, and led to the view that God's actions should *not* be unpredictable: since God is the custodian of natural law, divine action ought to be in strict conformity with that law, and thus not in conflict with any scientific discoveries. Surprisingly, a requirement to conform to scientific discovery does not, on its own, rule out the possibility of "special divine action" which overrides natural law. If such action took the form to manipulating a few molecules and then letting the result take effect strictly in accordance with natural laws, the initial manipulation would be undetectable by any scientific methods at present available, or likely to become so in the forseeable future. The outcome might be unusual, but since it would not be reproducable experimentally, it would be regarded as due to natural, random variation.

The second important change of classification in recent times has been the explanation of Bad intentions wholly in terms of human failure, or social influence, and not at all in terms of promptings by the Devil. The change is probably due mainly to increased understanding of motives, which can be shown to be based on normal human function even when they are unconscious. The seeming influence of personified evil in the non-material world, leading to Bad outcomes of Good intentions, has been reinterpreted as due to "misfortune" – that is complex factors, the joint operation of which is not predictable from present knowledge.

The concept of God developed in this chapter is in line with these changes, and further suggests that Good actions, and thus the activity of the Holy Spirit in man, are to be conceived in terms of elements in man's constitution which tend to guide his actions into conformity with what we have called basic reality. We shall see in the next chapter that this is not the same as saying that God is a projection of the conscience or super-ego (see Argyle, 1958, p. 155), but represents a more fundamental point of view. It is compatible with the idea that the Holy Spirit works strictly in accordance with the natural laws of brain and body, although as we have already noted, we have no means of proving that this is so.

It must be recognised that all the definitions of the "works of God" in the scheme we have outlined are inevitably circular. We regard a particular action as due to the work of God or the promptings of the Holy Spirit, because we have so defined a particular class of events or actions. This circularity is not, however, a ground for serious criticism. Many of the most important definitions in science are of the same type, and are thus in a sense unprovable. Their usefulness, like that of the concept of God, lies in the coherence and consistency they give to substantial bodies of facts.

JESUS CHRIST

The ideas about God that have been outlined here, lead readily to the concept of Christ as both fully man and fully God at the same time. As regards manhood, the accounts of Jesus in the Gospels give plenty of evidence of genuine Neutral actions, such as eating and drinking, and feelings of fatigue, pleasure, sorrow, joy and other emotions. As regards godhead, it seems fair to argue that men differ in the degree to which they perform Good actions as opposed to Bad, so that if a large group were studied, individuals would fall into a distribution from low, through medium to high in the proportion of Good actions they performed, and thus in the degree to which they possessed, or were possessed by, the Holy Spirit. Similar distributions of individuals are found for scores on intelligence and personality tests. Anyone so far out on the extreme of the distribution that he showed *only* Good or Neutral actions and *no* Bad ones, could in a very fair sense be regarded as completely possessed by the Holy Spirit, and if Jesus could be so described he would in an important sense be fully God. He might not necessarily be the complete and perfect manifestation of God, however, unless it could also be shown that, in his life and actions, he epitomised every possible type of Good action. We can fairly say that what we know of Jesus's life, and the fact that the principles he enunciated give a comprehensive guide to present-day living, suggest that this very stringent requirement is met, but we can never be absolutely sure that circumstances might not one day arise which would not be covered. The possibility is remote, but means that, strictly speaking, the concept of Jesus as the complete manifestation of God must be a working hypothesis —a matter of faith—rather than a conclusively proved fact. In this, it is like many important scientific theories.

The concept of Jesus' godhead that emerges from our discussion makes it possible to look afresh at some of the ideas which are, at present, felt by many to make Christianity unacceptable. We shall deal in turn with four: the suggestion that Jesus was a psychopath, miracles, virgin birth and Jesus as a sacrifice for the sins of the world.

Was Jesus a psychopath?

Several psychologists and psychiatrists have pointed to the fact that patients suffering from certain mental disorders often imagine themselves to be God, or some other prominent religious figure. From this they argue that Jesus, by claiming to be divine, was suffering from a disorder of this kind. The argument is superficial. Apart from the fact that there is no very good evidence that Jesus himself ever did claim to be divine — as opposed to dedicated — the patients concerned show little of the effectiveness and direction of ideas and behaviour that were shown by Jesus. For example, most of such patients are less than normally capable of looking after themselves, and their religious statements are little more than incoherent mumblings. Even if they are able to lead a life which approaches normal, their ideas turn out on close examination to be bizarre, and out of touch with reality in important respects. The view of God we have put forward implies that measuring up to reality is an important criterion of possession by the Holy Spirit, and thus of divinity. The effect that Jesus' life has had on the world indicates that he met this criterion well, so that even if he had claimed divinity, the claim would have been justified.

Miracles

One of the early assumptions made in order to ensure that Jesus was fully God, was that he had supernatural powers in relation to the natural environment, and was thus able to work miracles which ran counter to or interrupted natural law. Clearly, however, if what we have said about the nature of God is true, the ascription of miracles to Jesus is not necessary, and is indeed contradictory, since he epitomises the law that is being over-ridden. It is at the same time easy to see how the idea that Jesus worked miracles grew up. In New Testament times and before, miracles were regarded as an essential mark of divinity, and appear in the mythology of many religions. Stories handed on from one person to another have been shown to acquire very quickly a conventional form which accords with the expectations of hearers and the conventions of the society in which they live (Bartlett, 1932). The earliest of the Gospels, that of St. Mark, was not written until at least twenty years after Jesus' death, and much of it consists of stories which must have been handed down from mouth to mouth several times before they reached the author's hands. It is relevant to note that the one portion of the Gospel which has the ring of a first-hand, eye-witness account, is that of the Last Supper, Arrest and Cruci-fixion (Mark 14:12–15:41). These events, it has been suggested, were remembered directly by Mark who appears in the story as the young man fleeing naked from the Garden of Gethsemane when the soldiers tried to sieze him (Mark 14:51–52). All traces of miracle are conspicuously absent from this account, except for the reference to the veil of the Temple being torn in two (Mark 15:38). The verse containing this reference breaks the continuity of the story, and may well have been a later insertion. The corresponding accounts in St. Matthew's and St. Luke's Gospels, written a few years after St. Mark's and using it as a source, already show elements of miracle creeping in. According to St. Matthew, bodies rise from their graves when Jesus dies (Matthew 27:52), and in St. Luke's version, Jesus heals the ear of the High Priest's servant, which the other gospels merely say was cut off by one of Jesus' disciples (Luke 22:50–51).

Several attempts have been made to explain the Gospel miracles as natural events. Perhaps the simplest explanation derives from the fact that they were almost all cases of healing. Jesus was obviously a man of strong and attractive personality, with a quick and penetrating mind. We can also imagine him as possessed to an outstanding — it seemed to many a miraculous — degree, of the power shown by some psychiatrists and clinical psychologists to sort out people's troubles, and reorient their ideas, with a few kind but firm words. If so, many people who came to him in distress, will have gone away feeling that a great weight of anxiety and guilt had rolled away from them, and many mental and psychosomatic disorders will have quickly cleared up.

Virgin Birth

A further early attempt to ensure the full godhead of Jesus was based on a biological assumption which is now known to be false. Until comparatively recent years, it was commonly assumed that, in conception, the male planted seed in the female, who supplied it with the sustenance needed for growth and development, but nothing more. Jesus was thus regarded as obtaining his godhead from the seed implanted by the Holy Spirit, and his manhood from the sustenance derived from Mary his mother. We now know, of course, that conception occurs from the union of a male sperm and female ovum, so that both contribute equally to the hereditary make-up of the offspring. If, therefore, Jesus' birth was really as described in St. Matthew's and St. Luke's Gospels (Matthew 1:18–20; Luke 1:28–35) Jesus would have been in a sense *half* God and *half* man.

It is true that subsequent virgin births have been reported from time to time, but those investigated carefully seem to have been unconvincing. In any case, the view of God and Jesus we have put forward, makes the doctrine of the Virgin Birth redundant. To assume that Jesus was conceived naturally by two human parents in no way affects the idea that he was completely possessed of, and by, the Holy Spirit, while it preserves his full manhood in a way that the traditional doctrine cannot.

Jesus as a sacrifice for the sins of the world

The concept of Jesus as saviour is obvious for those who accept that the ideas he enunciated and demonstrated, can transform an unsatisfying and worthless life into a profoundly satisfying and valuable one. However what, if any, psychological

THE CONCEPT OF GOD

justification is there for the seemingly primitive view that Jesus, by his death on the Cross, made a sacrifice of himself which can expurgate the sins of the whole world? Sacrifice in primitive religions seems to have had two main aims: the partaking of a meal in common with a god, and giving a present to a god in order to atone for wrongdoing or secure a favour. It seems to be a natural human characteristic, although one which differs in strength between individuals, to feel guilt at actions which are regarded as wrong, and to seek to make restitution. If the person wronged is present to receive restitution, or if a poorly performed task can have its shortcomings repaired, the feelings of guilt can be dissipated. If, however, restitution is impossible, a kind of substitute restitution may be attempted by giving away a treasured possession, or undertaking a painful or unpleasant task as a penance.

A child in a loving home will experience many occasions on which a parent will either make restitution or undergo suffering on its behalf, and will thus gain the idea that other people's sacrifices can atone for one's own wrongdoing. Such thinking is possibly enhanced by the common human tendency to generalise from the individual to the group, so that a whole group acquires praise or blame from the activities of one or a few members. We thus speak of a whole country as having won a war, or even a football match. This kind of thinking seems often to have occurred among religious people, not only in biblical times, but even up to the present day. It is, for example, only recently that the Roman Catholic Church has officially declared that present-day Jews are no longer to be held guilty for Jesus' Crucifixion.

The idea that Jesus' death can make amends for our own day-to-day wrongdoing, may give relief to some whose sense of guilt is over-active, but seems incomprehensible in any literal sense. It is, however, more understandable if we look at it step by step in two ways. First, Jesus by his life showed us how to live and to overcome the human limitations that lead to wrong-doing: at the same time, the principles by which he lived made his crucifixion inevitable. Therefore, the Crucifixion was an essential part of the example he has provided for us, and is thus a *symbol* which epitomises the example. Second, the Crucifixion brought home to the world as nothing else could, the value of the principles Jesus stood for. It thus led to these principles being incorporated into the culture in which we have grown up —a culture which, without its deep Christian background, would be very much harsher than it is today. The Crucifixion is thus the *cause* of our world being better than it would otherwise have been.

This way of looking at Jesus' sacrifice, enables us to understand what is, for many people, a difficult problem regarding the Eucharist. What do we mean by eating bread and drinking wine as the body and blood of Jesus? Did Jesus at the Last Supper endorse the traditional idea of sacrifice? Many Christian thinkers have held that he did, and that it is necessary to define a way in which the bread and wine are miraculously transformed into the genuine flesh and blood of Jesus. Such a view seems to reflect the tendency to concrete thinking and away from figurative statements we noted earlier in this chapter (p. 53). The simplest interpretation of Jesus' words as reported in the Gospels suggests a different view. They seem plausibly to mean something like this: "The principles and ideas I have taught and lived for, hold the key to man's future well-being; they also lead inevitably to my death. There is thus a sense in which I can be said to be a sacrifice for mankind's future. Yet this is really only a symbol of the dedication that everyone needs to make every day. Therefore think of this bread and wine—everyday food and drink—as symbolic of my sacrifice, and re-dedicate yourselves each time you partake of them."

Jesus' life

The Gospels as we have them are a mixture of history and
legend, of eye-witness accounts and hearsay, of direct memory
and the end products of traditions handed down by word of
mouth for between a quarter and three quarters of a century.
All have almost certainly been subject to the selection, rational-
isation, changes of emphasis and distortion into conformity
with the expectations, hopes, fears and general manner of
thinking of the time. We cannot recover many of the original
events with much confidence, but we can attempt, from what
we know of human memory, to extrapolate backwards from
the accounts we now have to a tentative sketch of Jesus' life.
This we shall attempt to do briefly as a means of summing up
the ideas that have been advanced here, painting a picture the
outlines of which were sketched in a fascinating little book by
Burkitt (1932).

Jesus as a boy, we may imagine, showed an early interest in
religion. There was a ferment of thought at the time about how
men ought to live, about the doctrines and purposes of the
Jewish Law, and about the possibility of a Messiah coming to
deliver Israel from Roman rule. Jesus thought deeply about
these problems and, living in the north of the country, was
probably less influenced than he might otherwise have been by
the strictly orthodox, conservative ideas emanating from the
Temple at Jerusalem. He was interested in John the Baptist's
teaching and probably discussed it with him. John was im-
pressed by Jesus, and perhaps urged him that he should put
his ideas forward publicly, as they were much more positive
than his own, and might indeed prove the salvation of the nation.

Jesus retires to the wilderness to ponder what he should do,
and works out a plan of action. As a first principle, he must set
out to convince by argument, and by the sheer quality of his

teaching and the sincerity of his life, rather than by any spectacular or forcible means. He thus begins his preaching mission. Various experiences during it link in his mind with some of the Old Testament prophecies, and he gradually comes to realise that he might, in a sense, indeed be the Messiah – not as a military leader to throw off Roman occupation by force, but as a teacher of how men can live in such a way that any disadvantages of such rule are of no real significance. The idea of Messiahship is confirmed by Peter's recognition of him as Christ.

So far as Jesus' own emotional satisfaction was concerned, Peter's recognition was probably the high point of his career. Despite his powerful and magnetic personality, and the faith he inspired in many of his listeners, his teaching had a mixed reception. He came gradually to realise that he might have to suffer if there was to be any hope of getting his message across, and would need to concentrate his efforts on an inner circle of followers, who could carry on after him if his own career was cut short. He makes a last bid to sway opinion on a large scale by riding into Jerusalem in a manner such as to fulfil another Old Testament prophecy, and by making an outspoken stand against the corruption and commercialism in the Temple precincts. The attempt fails, however, and when the end comes, he dies with the words on his lips: "Oh God, why have you abandoned me?"

From our point of view, the precise details of Jesus' life are perhaps not really important. What matters to us is that all the decisions he took appear to have been right in their intentions and, as subsequent events seem to have shown, right also in their outcome.

This brief sketch leaves out of account one further matter which, from a Christian standpoint is important. The Resurrection of Jesus, compared with the Crucifixion, is not well documented. The accounts in the various Gospels do not agree. Those in St. Mark are obviously a later addition, replacing a continuation beyond verse 8 of chapter 16 which seems to have been lost in the early days of the church. Obviously *something* took place which made Jesus' followers believe that he was alive and led them to act accordingly, with results that still affect us today. We shall probably never know exactly what happened. For example, it is medically plausible to suggest that Jesus did not really die on the Cross but fainted, and may thus well have recovered after being taken down. One cannot even rule out the possibility that, in what we speak of as the resurrection appearances, Jesus was impersonated by someone else, perhaps as part of a scheme of stage-management engineered by influential people such as Joseph of Arimathea. This, if it were true, would make sense of some curious features of the resurrection accounts, such as the failure by two disciples on their way to Emmaus to recognise Jesus when he walked with them. (Luke, 24:13–35).

Two further points about the Resurrection must be mentioned briefly. First, Jesus' resurrection, in whatever sense it occurred, may suggest the possibility of an after-life for others, but does not prove it. As a point of historical fact, the belief in an after-life in which the just are rewarded and sinners are punished came relatively late in Jewish religion, not being at all generally accepted until after about 200 B.C. Second, belief in the death and resurrection of a god is not unique to Christianity: it occurs in many religions, and would have had a much greater significance in Jesus' time than it would have today. The initial appeal of Jesus as God might well have failed, had there not been some event which could be interpreted as a resurrection. On a lesser scale, we can all think of politicians whose acceptability is enhanced by, according to party, their military or trade-union record.

Whether or not doubts about the traditional interpretation of the Resurrection are justified, they do not, on the views we have outlined in this chapter, detract from the importance and nature of Jesus as God and Messiah. Resurrection in the gross literalness of flesh and bones is not necessary to the validity of the Christian way of looking at life and the world. Jesus' importance lies essentially in the ideas and principles he enunciated in his teaching and demonstrated in his life, and in his willingness to face death. These remain, whatever view is taken of the Crucifixion and of the events which followed.

Chapter IV

Frameworks of Purpose

TAKING of action obviously requires a degree of mental and physical capacity, together with an appropriate opportunity. These, however, are not enough: there must also be some *drive* or *motive*. Thus, for example, the capacity to eat, coupled with the presence of food, is not enough to ensure that eating will occur: there must also be hunger or some social pressure to partake. It has often been argued that these motives can all be traced back, directly or indirectly, to primary biological necessities for either the individual, such as eating, or the race, such as sexual intercourse and the nurturing of young. This view is, however, difficult to sustain for two types of reason. First, people do not normally eat in order to preserve life or engage in sexual activity with a view to preserving the race. Motives are usually of a more sensual nature: we eat because of sensations of hunger, and enjoy food for its taste, smell and appearance; and these sensory gratifications satisfy our hunger long before the food has been digested and become available to nourish the body. Second, play activities, interests in work or hobbies, and desires for social contacts seem far removed from any biological necessities for survival.

A way out of these difficulties is provided by the evidence which has been accumulating in recent years that, underlying both biological and social motives, there is a fundamental motivating principle that animals, including man, *attempt to secure results from action* — in other words they try to obtain

73

feedback (see Woodworth, 1958, Welford, 1968, chapter 10). Motivation arises because we find ourselves in a situation in which, by taking action, we can achieve results. We therefore act, and by so doing, modify the situation until it ceases to provide the opportunity to secure further results.

Such a view of motivation makes it an example of a servo-mechanism, and analogous to the ship's power-assisted steering gear mentioned in Chapter 1 (p. 15). The ship's steering-engine comes into operation as soon as there is any discrepancy between the positions of the rudder and the wheel on the bridge, and continues to operate to turn the rudder until the discrepancy is abolished. In the same way, we can say that when hunger arises we eat until it is satisfied, and that we pursue games, hobbies or social contacts until some result has been achieved, either to ourselves or to the world around us. The analogy can be pressed in the sense that, just as the speed of the steering-engine depends on the extent of the misalignment between rudder and wheel, so if an animal is deprived of food, water or air, its actions become more and more vigorous as the deprivation becomes more acute, until physical exhaustion supervenes. Similarly, in a number of more complex human activities such as problem-solving, the intensity of effort rises with increased incentive, sometimes to such a level that performance is actually impaired by over-excitement and anxiety.

Three elaborations to the servo-model are, however, necessary. First, several variables may combine to determine the effective stimulus to action. In particular, the incentive effect of a potential reward or successful outcome is partly offset by the cost in terms of effort, difficulty or unpleasantness involved in achieving it. Readiness to undertake an action may, therefore, be conceived as depending on some kind of *ratio*, or *difference*, between *result* and *cost*. Such a relationship provides an obvious explanation of the common reluctance to undertake laborious or difficult tasks, and also suggests a reason for certain types of delinquent behaviour such as stealing, since this is usually easier than earning, and vandalism, since a much greater ratio of effect to effort is usually produced by destruction than by constructive activities. On the other hand, the expenditure of effort seems to make the result appear more valuable (for a review see Lewis, 1965), and an ability acquired laboriously tends to be regarded as more potentially useful than one which has come easily (Yaryan & Festinger, 1961). By the same tokens, an activity abandoned in the face of a threat, appears to be more desirable if the threat has been severe than if it has been mild (Aronson & Carlsmith, 1963).

Second, a distinction needs to be drawn between cases in which each action taken reduces to some extent the conditions which initiated activity, and cases in which a whole chain of actions has to be completed before any reduction is achieved. To the former, the simple servo-model applies well, in the sense that motivation tends to diminish as activity proceeds: we all know, for example, how the rate of eating declines towards the end of a large meal, and how difficult it is to persuade a builder to finish off the last details of a house, once it is habitable. When results follow only after a chain of actions, however, the speed and vigour of performance tend gradually to increase up to the point at which the goal is attained and action ceases. Why this happens is not at present clear, and any or all of several possible reasons may be true. The classical explanation is based on the finding from many experiments, that the incentive value of a reward diminishes if it is not given until some time after completion of the achievement which has earned it. Most of the evidence that this is so comes from work with animals, but the same results have been shown for human beings (e.g. Mischel *et al.* 1969). On this view the gap, in terms of time or intervening events, before obtaining the reward is relatively great at the beginning of the task, so that the incentive effect of the reward is low. As the task proceeds, the gap shortens and the incentive effect rises correspondingly.

Two other possible explanations are, however, worth noting. One is that, at the beginning of a long chain of actions, the effort to be expended before the final result is achieved is large, but that it progressively diminishes as the task proceeds. On this view, the increase of performance as the final result is approached, is another effect of the relationship between result achieved and cost of achieving it. The other explanation lies in the fact that observing the results of one's actions seems to be a spur to further action. At first sight, this may seem to run counter to the servo-principle. The time-scale is, however, different. Knowledge that an action has achieved its goal leads to the cessation of that particular action, but it also has an enlivening effect which encourages activity in general and the making of further actions of the same kind, and thus the continuation of a repetitive task. For example, Gibbs & Brown (1956) found that the rate at which a photo-copying machine was operated, increased when a counter was mounted on it, showing the number of documents copied. On this basis, knowledge that the goal was being approached should have a stimulating effect, which would progressively enhance performance so long as the conditions originally giving rise to it remained in being. All these explanations can account for the well-known difficulty of taking action before the need for it has become pressing.

The third elaboration of the servo-model that we need to take into account is that, in any real-life performance, there are not one but many servo-loops operating simultaneously. Consider, for example, the skilled turner in an engineering workshop. As he moves the tool of his lathe over the face of a casting, he has to co-ordinate and order a series of actions which jointly accomplish the task of machining the face concerned. This series, however, is only one of several involved in the larger task of machining the whole casting, and the casting may be only one of several required for a single job of construction. There are, in short, a whole hierarchy of tasks of different magnitudes and time-scales of which the larger embrace the smaller, co-ordinate them, and in a real sense provide the immediate motives for them.

The hierarchical principle does not stop at the individual unit of production. If we were to ask the turner why he was engaged on his job of construction, he might reply that it was part of his work at the factory, that this in turn was a means of earning a high wage, that his earnings would enable him to buy a car, and that this would enhance the opportunities enjoyed by his family. The higher orders of these tasks tend to be of a social nature while the lower are more individual, but they shade into each other without any marked discontinuity.

We may note immediately several important implications of this hierarchical principle. First, it is easy to understand how one action may result from several motives working together: for example, we may go to a concert partly because we like music, partly because we know people we want to see are going to be there, and partly because we feel the need for a break from what we have been doing during the past week or so. Second, the motive behind a particular activity may change with time: for instance, a man may join a sports club because he enjoys exercise, and may continue for the sake of the friend-ships he has formed. Third, the same motive may produce several different actions: the single overall aim of producing this book has involved, at different times, looking up and reading source material, writing several drafts of the text, checking references, correcting proofs, and a host of minor tasks. Fourth, the pursuit of a longer-term task may give rise to behaviour which would otherwise be avoided. Grimble (1953) tells the story of how, when he was a District Officer in the Gilbert Islands, his wife gave lessons in mothercraft to some pregnant women serving sentences in the local prison: as a result, several expectant mothers deliberately committed crimes in order to get into prison and thus be able to attend the lessons. Similarly, many tramps commit minor offences in mid-December in order to obtain the comforts of prison for Christmas.

The longest term tasks shade into general principles of living, and lend continuity to the aims a person sets himself in daily life. The goals of these tasks often cannot be located at any particular time in the future, and may indeed lie beyond the individual's own span of life – as when someone sets out on a programme of research or a policy of reform which he knows he will not finish, but hopes will be completed by his successors. Nevertheless the goals are, in the terms we have been using, long-term tasks, and the individual's pattern of life would change markedly if they either were achieved or had to be abandoned.

CONTROL OF MOTIVES

Action that any reasonable person would regard as sound, wise or right, clearly requires that certain motives are sometimes overridden. There are many situations in which we have to do what we do not immediately wish to, as when we have to eat out of politeness even though we are not hungry, or have to carry out tedious exercises in the course of school or university studies. We often have to undertake relatively unrewarding tasks which are nevertheless difficult. We may have to set out vigorously on activities which take a long time, or require a great deal of work, before they yield any result. This last seems to be especially prominent in tasks which require the exercise of *responsibility* which, it has been suggested, can be defined in terms of the length of time over which action has to be taken without supervisory check or other indication of its success (Jaques, 1956).

In some cases, the immediate result is worth the cost, as when the anticipated pleasure of seeing a play makes it seem worth waiting in a queue for a ticket. In most cases, however, our willingness to set aside immediate motives can be traced to the fact that longer term tasks not only contain shorter ones, but also *control* them. At an elementary level, several studies have shown that, in cases like the turner we mentioned, the overall requirements of a job determine the tempo, accuracy, order and manner in which constituent actions are carried out. In the same way, the wider social tasks may determine priorities, such as that money shall be saved for a car instead of being spent on entertainment, or that a job shall be chosen which offers high wages and overtime rather than comfort or security. In short, the higher-order tasks can make sub-tasks worthwhile by giving them a place in a wider context, even though they would not be undertaken for their own sake.

Ability to work on a long time-scale in this way confers an important biological advantage, in the sense that larger scale operations can be undertaken and problems dealt with at arm's length before they become pressing. Such ability seems to be a mark of advancement in the animal kingdom. For example, a rat or a dog will work for food if it is hungry, but cannot, like a chimpanzee, be trained to work for tokens that have to be kept until later to be exchanged for food. Obviously man is, in this respect, in an altogether superior position to other animals, but even within the human species, gradations can be seen between those who tend to live for the moment, and those who plan ahead. Thus if children are given the choice of an immediate, smaller reward, or a larger reward after a wait of a fortnight or so, for successfully completing a task, those who choose the delayed rewards tend to have a longer time-perspective — they are able to look ahead further and remember back more accurately than those who choose immediate rewards. They also tend to have higher intelligence scores, to be older, to be more socially responsible, and not to be delinquent (Mischel, 1961, Mischel & Metzner, 1962).

Right action, in the sense of action which is in line with the basic realities of nature and the world — in line with what Christians call the "Will of God" — appears therefore to be mainly concerned with the choice of appropriate high-level, long-term tasks or aims in life. If such tasks are chosen well, they can co-ordinate and give direction to the lesser tasks of day-to-day living, enabling what would be in itself distasteful or tedious to be done willingly, providing a steady aim which can overcome temporary setbacks and disappointments, and making full and efficient use of individual capacities. From a traditional Christian point of view, it should be emphasised that the full achievement of these aims may not occur in our lifetime. However, satisfaction seems often to depend on the knowledge that a worthwhile aim is being pursued, rather than on the final achievement of the goal, so that faith in the value of one's aim is more important than belief in personal reward after death.

The importance of long-term aims does not mean that more immediate bodily and emotional needs should be ignored. Our capacities are often much greater than we realise, but they are limited, and if they are pushed beyond their limits, performance will be inefficient and less than fully effective. Thus, excessive stress, effort, asceticism or self-denial, especially if continuous and unrelenting, not only lead to an uninspiring life, but can impair bodily health and mental efficiency. We need to aim high, but not impossibly high, and to have some relaxation, pleasure and even some indulgences, if we are to realise our full potential. One of the most frequent histories of students who break down at university, is of parents, teachers or both having maintained a severe and unrelenting pressure to achieve high results, and as each result has come along, allowed no period of rejoicing and relaxation, but immediately raised the sights and looked forward to the student's next task ahead.

Conscience

An individual judges the rightness or wrongness of any desire or action by comparing it with a framework of principles based on the teaching of parents and others. This framework was termed the "super-ego" by Freud, and is more familiarly recognised as *conscience*. Research into the origins of conscience has been lucidly surveyed by Argyle (1961), who notes that strength of conscience, as indicated by intensity of guilt feelings when it is disobeyed, is associated with the style of parental discipline. Conscience tends to be more powerful if disapproval has been shown by withdrawal of affection rather than by either severe corporal punishment (Sears *et al.* 1957) or withdrawal of material rewards (Grusec, 1966). For children old enough to understand, explanation of the consequences of wrong action seems to be even more effective than withdrawal of affection (Hoffman & Saltzstein, 1967). The tendency for these less severe punishments to be used more in middle-class than working-class homes may partly account for the finding that middle-class children tend to have a better-developed moral sense than those from working-class homes (Aronfreed, 1961), although the greater sensitivity and thoughtful care that middle-class mothers tend to show, is probably also important.

All this is not to say that other styles of punishment are ineffective: for example, occasional intense punishments consisting of a firm "NO" accompanied by a loud noise, have in certain circumstances been found to be successful, and more so than frequent mild punishments (Leff, 1969). Other suggestions have been that guilt feelings at disobeying conscience, depend more upon the affection or approval felt by the child for the parent who does the disciplining, than for the type of discipline used (Jourard, 1954, Moulton *et al.* 1966), and that need for approval is more important than punishment – guilt feelings tend to be found most among those with very high or very low desires for approval (Bethlehem, 1969). Argyle notes that the dictates of conscience tend to follow principles taken over by boys from their fathers and by girls from their mothers, and suggests that the fact that young children normally have more contact with their mothers than their fathers, is the reason why girls have frequently been found to have more active consciences than boys. It may also be the reason why they are more severe in their moral judgements (e.g. Eisenman, 1967, Wright & Cox, 1967b).

Parental discipline is not the only factor engendering conscience and shaping moral judgements. For example, Piaget (1932) has argued that, as a child grows up, he sometimes finds moral standards inculcated by his parents in disagreement with those of his peers, and that he builds up a moral code in the course of resolving these conflicts (see also Haan *et al.* 1968). Again, religious affiliation is associated with somewhat stricter moral judgements (e.g. Haimes & Hetherington, 1964, Klinger *et al.*, 1964, Wright & Cox, 1967b), which tend to follow the doctrines of different denominations (London *et al.* 1964), and to change as these change: for instance, a study has shown that in the course of the Second Vatican Œcumenical Council, a sample of Roman Catholic students became more favourable to birth control and less anti-semitic than they had been before (Ward & Barrett, 1968).

Conscience has been shown, in several studies, to have a range of associated effects. It has been found, for example, that feelings of guilt lead to greater compliance to the wishes of others (Freedman *et al.* 1967) and, surprisingly, to a tendency to overvalue objects acquired dishonestly (Brock, 1963); also that resistance to temptations to cheat are associated with better attention to an experimental task, greater exercise of restraint and lower levels of restlessness (Grim *et al.* 1968). There are, however, considerable variations: for instance, both conformity and protest can emanate from conscientious views firmly held by different individuals (Haan *et al.* 1968), and the effects of various influences which shape conscience differ according to the sex, personality and social class of the child and his relations with his parents (Argyle & Delin, 1965). Also, the situations which stir conscience differ between individuals (MacRae, 1954, Black & London, 1966), and correlations between moral judgement and feelings of guilt are by no means perfect (Ruma & Mosher, 1967).

The evidence we have surveyed regarding the origins and effects of conscience, indicate that it is a frame of reference built up in the course of experience. While its foundations are laid in early childhood, it is liable to change to some extent as experience brings better understanding of events, more accurate appraisal of the likely outcome of actions, and the need to resolve conflicts; and as the goals of life are either achieved or abandoned. Such changes usually occur slowly, however, so that the dictates of conscience tend to lag behind the requirements of the present situation. The important conclusion therefore emerges, that conscience cannot be regarded as the infallible inner voice of God. However valuable it may be as a means of co-ordinating and stabilising behaviour, it is subject to error and is thus in need of continual checking against the best that we know, or can discover, of the broader framework of what we have called basic reality. Such checks are essential if outdated requirements and prohibitions are to be abandoned, and new ones made necessary by fresh circumstances are to be incorporated.

Sin

The conclusion we have reached on conscience has implications regarding the centuries-old conflict of view among religious thinkers, about whether sin consists of acting against conscience or against basic reality. Clearly the latter is the more fundamental definition since it is, in principle, capable of objective, precise specification, subject only to the availability of knowledge, whereas conscience is liable to individual error from many sources. However, it is fair to argue that insofar as conscience has been trained and disciplined by careful thought, it is an indicator of when sin may have occurred, or be about to occur, and that it is therefore, a useful if not infallible guide.

Christian doctrine has laid considerable stress upon the idea that man is "born in sin" — that is, naturally sinful. In the terms we have been using, this is true in two ways. First, man does not automatically and naturally conform to basic reality: instead his actions are inevitably conditioned by his knowledge, and this in turn by the state of insight attained by the society in which he lives. He therefore sins in an objective sense through sheer ignorance, however hard he may try not to do so. Second, even if he does know what action is likely to be in conformity with basic reality, his immediate biological desires may in certain circumstances be so strong that they cannot be set aside or controlled.

What Christian doctrine has not recognised so explicitly is that, although these human characteristics appear at first sight to be serious deficiencies, as compared with those of a race of supermen so constituted by nature that they always automatically did what was right, they are in fact the basis of man's potentiality for progress. Such imperfections, when coupled with insight into the fact that they are imperfections, provide the essential conditions for discovery of the nature of the universe and of things and people in it, and for using these discoveries to master nature. If error never occurred, man would have no need for insight into the world and its workings, and would probably have no conscious awareness of them. Conscious insight seems to be concerned essentially with the resolution of uncertainty. Thus, when we go through the motions of a routine, familiar task, we have little awareness of the details of what we are doing: our consciousness is concentrated upon some broader aspect of our work, such as wondering whether we shall get the job done in time, and only returns to the details of what we are doing if something goes wrong.

It follows from what we have just said, that a life without problems, effort and struggle would be an essentially vegetative existence, which might be without pain and suffering, but would equally be without satisfactions since there would be no challenge, and therefore no conscious awareness. If so, a new light is shed on the statement "In the sweat of thy face shalt thou eat bread" made to Adam and Eve in the Garden of Eden (Genesis 3:19). The author of the story seems to have regarded it as a curse for disobeying God by eating the fruit of the tree of knowledge, and as signifying man's hard lot in the world. Yet today we can see that it might be more accurately construed as a promise: "If you undertake the struggle involved in grappling with the world and its problems, you will not only obtain a material living, but will also gain knowledge of the truth."

85

Motives lead to actions, and the effectiveness of repeated actions gradually improves because we learn from our success and failure on previous occasions. In short, we acquire skills which enable us to recognise the meanings of events, and give us the techniques for dealing with them. When the same situation occurs many times, such skills become habitual, and our actions take on a relatively stereotyped form. Yet skills are more than fixed routines. The skilled operator is able not only to deal better than the unskilled with situations he has met before, but is also better able to deal with novel situations for which he has no ready-made routine, but has to construct one specially. This is, however, more difficult than repeating what has been done before, and tends to be avoided if possible. Activities thus tend to fall into a repeated pattern, which fits the situation reasonably well so long as it does not change to any great extent. If it does change, or if the operator gains new insight into its requirements, the habitual pattern of action will no longer suffice. If the changes or insights come slowly and are of small extent, the routine can be gradually and progressively modified, but if they come faster, or are of a more radical nature, the old routine may have to be abandoned and a new one substituted.

Very much the same kind of process seems to underlie the changes in the patterns of living, or long-term tasks of life, that have come to be known as religious *conversion*. This was extensively studied by several research workers concerned with the psychology of religion during the early years of the century, following the classical work of Starbuck (1899) who examined some two thousand cases. He found that the frequency of conversions rose to a peak in the middle teens. It seemed as if the growing insights and awakening powers of these years, made the aims and patterns of life built up in childhood no longer adequate, and that conversion marked an attempt to bring them into line with the new requirements. For some, the change was gradual, brought about by a series of piecemeal adjustments which caused little difficulty or distress. For others, the change was more violent: at first they clung to their former way of life, while becoming acutely aware of the discrepancy between it and their present needs, so that they suffered distressing feelings of inadequacy, doubt, alienation, guilt and sinfulness. Eventually they abandoned their old way and embraced a new, often to the accompaniment of an emotional crisis. After the change, they commonly experienced exaggerated feelings of virtue, joy, peace and "oneness with God".

The sudden changes often came about at a revival meeting or religious service, but were frequently precipitated by seemingly trivial events which had little bearing on the situation. It was, however, clear from the preceding state of worry and distress, that these sudden changes had been in preparation for a considerable time before they actually arrived, and that the precipitating events were essentially triggers rather than causes. They were analogous to the seemingly trivial facts or events which can upon occasion suddenly precipitate the solution to a problem we have been grappling with unsuccessfully for a long time. In the subject's conscious experience, the change usually seemed to be much more radical than it appeared to an external observer, and was often unstable, being followed in some cases by a further change, and in others by a partial or complete swing back to former ideas. Such relapses back seemed to be especially common following conversion at revival meetings. One may suspect that at these, subjects had been carried away by emotions into accepting propositions which turned out on further examination to be incompatible with their previous framework of ideas, and insufficiently coherent to act as replacements.

Although conversion is commonly regarded as an important type of religious experience, which is often equated with the "second birth" mentioned in the New Testament, it is not confined to religion. Similar conversion experiences can occur in relation to systems of secular beliefs, including the typical feelings of disquiet beforehand, emotional crisis at the time of change from one set of beliefs to another, and exaggerated joy afterwards. There is, therefore, nothing specifically religious in a conversion experience as such: its religious significance must lie in the system of ideas involved in the change, and in the effects of the change upon behaviour.

A second caution against laying undue stress on conversion experiences lies in the fact that they are associated with denomination: members of some denominations tend to experience sudden, crisis-type conversions, while members of others go through more gradual realignments of their religious ideas. Why these differences exist is not clear. They have traditionally been attributed to social influences exerted by the congregation of which the individual is a member, but this merely shifts the question to that of why one congregation should exert a particular influence while another does not. We shall see in the next chapter that the members of various denominations tend to differ in a number of ways, and some of these would be sufficient to account for the association between denomination and conversion. For example, clinging to a system of beliefs, despite mounting evidence that it is inadequate, is a mark of "rigidity" of personality, which in turn is associated with relatively low intelligence, and particularly with stress, anxiety and an austere approach to life. It is, therefore, not surprising that crisis-type conversions tend to occur among those strict evangelical sects which minister to rather special groups of people whose origins are humble, but who are extremely anxious to maintain respectability, and tend to live under some stress in doing so. The same association would be predicted by the finding that the tendency to make definite as opposed to tentative assertions, seemingly reflecting a desire for certainty, varies between individuals and is greater under conditions of frustration and stress (Brim & Hoff, 1957). The crisis-type of conversion can be regarded as due to the subject not being able to tolerate having his system of beliefs in disarray – he must be certain about them all, and therefore clings to his old system until a new one is fully formed. If so, this type of conversion would tend to occur among those who were especially frustrated – which we have seen in Chapter II the members of extreme evangelical sects tend to be.

FAITH

Accounts of conversion experiences frequently speak of the subject's feeling that he was "losing his faith" before the crisis, and that he had gained or regained it after. This finding is in line with the point implied in the first chapter, that only a small part of our ideas and beliefs can be based on scientific proof or direct experience: much has to be taken on trust from others. In accepting it, we tend to take over a system of beliefs more or less whole, since it is only by doing so that we can quickly acquire a coherent framework within which to live. The consequence is that we often have to act on unverified information, and take decisive action although we are unable to be sure that it is well directed. Essentially the same problem arises over certain of the motivational situations outlined at the beginning of this chapter: whenever a series of actions has to be taken before a result can be observed, as in the performance of long-term tasks, we have to commit ourselves to action in anticipation of an outcome which we cannot be sure will occur. For example, a student studying for an end-of-year examination, has to go through a whole year's programme of work before he has any certain knowledge of whether he is undertaking it in an adequate manner. He has to make what is, in Christian terms, an *act of faith*, not knowing whether what he does will be successful, but working on the assumption that it will be. It must be recognised that only such an act of faith can make success possible: the student who argued that he could not work because he did not know whether he was good enough to pass the examination at the end of the year, would inevitably fail. The Christian way of life has always stressed an active, outgoing attitude to the world and its problems so that faith, as a means of securing and fostering human endeavour, has understandably been a central principle of Christianity.

Taking decisive action on the basis of uncertain information is an emotionally exacting task, and seems often to cause attempts to raise confidence by regarding the information as more reliable than it in fact is. We should expect this to be especially likely to occur when, as is often the case with religious behaviour, the grounds on which action has to be taken are impossible to verify in any direct way, so that the outcome of action cannot be predicted with confidence. Thouless (1935) and Brown (1962) verified that this tendency did occur, in studies in which they asked subjects to state the certainty of different kinds of belief. They presented a series of statements, some of which were factual and secular, such as "Hornets live in nests under the ground"; and some were religious, such as "The world was created by God". They found that subjects tended to believe or disbelieve the statements strongly, rather than express doubt or uncertainty. This was true of most of the statements they used, but especially so of the religious ones.

The tendency did not differ with intelligence or sex, and was present equally among both religious believers and disbelievers. The present writer found the same trend towards certainty also in statements about religious behaviour (Welford, 1959). Subjects were presented with a short account of a man losing his job in middle age when it might be difficult to find another, and were asked to record the certainty with which they would, if they were the man concerned, take each of several non-religious actions, such as registering with an employment agency or seeking out possible employers, and also whether they would pray for help or peace of mind. The certainty with which people indicated they would, or would not, pray was much greater than that with which they indicated they would take other forms of action.

These findings tally well with everyday experience. It is the propositions about which we are doubtful, but on which we have to take decisive action, that we tend most vehemently to assert to be true – or false. Our behaviour in this respect is paradoxical, in the sense that outward certainty implies inward doubt: insofar as it is difficult to live with doubt, we try to get rid of it, and if this cannot be done by obtaining definite information, we tend to behave as if the uncertainty was not there. In the religious sphere, this is in line with the evidence regarding frustration and desire for certainty mentioned in connection with conversion: it is this desire for certainty that can reasonably be supposed to cause the powerful, assertive preaching and insistence that the Bible is in all respects literally true, that are commonly found with extreme evangelical sects. They speak as they do, because their faith is actually less secure than that of more questioning and doubting, yet more genuinely confident, Christians of other denominations.

Chapter V

The Church

E VERY religion which is not purely private to an individual, must have some organisation for the propagation and preservation of its values, ideals and traditions. Such an organisation can be regarded as a kind of corporate embodiment of these principles, giving them actuality insofar as they are expressed and exercised by its members. In this sense, the Church can be said to embody Christianity collectively, just as Jesus is held to have done so in his individual person. If so, it is not, perhaps, too far-fetched to describe the Church as the "Body of Christ", although the metaphor appears somewhat highly coloured for this day and age.

Organisation implies social interaction between individuals, so that we should expect that a range of principles belonging to social psychology would apply to the Church. These should help us to understand the way in which it grew up, and have lessons to teach about its present functioning and future development.

CHARACTERISTICS OF SOCIAL GROUPS

The meaning attached to the term "group" varies in different contexts. For example, physical anthropologists may group men according to the shape of their skulls, while those concerned with employment may think of occupational groups and divide men according to their trade, degree of training or extent of responsibility. The social psychologist, however, uses the term "group" or "social group" in a more restricted sense, to denote an association of people who have a degree of coherence or unity. For people to form a group in this sense, two conditions must be fulfilled: first they must have *something in common* which they believe to be of significance to them; and second their association together must in some way be to their *mutual advantage*, either because they benefit positively by acting together, or because there would be sanctions against them if they did not. Both conditions appear to be necessary. For example, men with fair hair do not form a psychological group, because the possession of fair hair does not significantly affect their lives; while women who might feel that being blonde did make a difference, nevertheless do not form a coherent group because there is no advantage to them in doing so, and nobody seeks to compel them. On the other hand, racial minorities, such as negroes in America, do tend to cohere because they feel their skin colour places them at a disadvantage, which can be minimised if they take joint action.

We shall consider these two conditions as they relate to the Church, taking for convenience the second of them first.

Benefits of group membership

Most groups in real life do not exist on their own, but as members of a hierarchy of groups of different sizes, the larger embracing the smaller. Thus in the Church of England, the parish congregations to which individuals belong are grouped into Dioceses, these again into Archiepiscopal Provinces, and the Provinces together make up the Anglican Communion. Groups at the base of such a hierarchy tend to be more coherent than those at higher levels, their impact on individuals is more direct, and the effects of membership are more immediate. In terms of the motivational principles set out at the beginning of the previous chapter, we should expect such directness and immediacy to have a motivating effect, so that individuals would derive greater satisfaction from membership of these smaller groups, than of those which are larger but exert less direct influence. In the case of the Church this means that, although it may be inspiring to belong to a world-wide organisation, the main ties which bind people to the Church as a whole must come from local services and parish activities. If, and only if, these satisfy a genuine need, will the higher levels of the Church be strong.

The basic attraction of church services for individuals is probably not the reviewing of Christian principles and opportunity for realignment of oneself with basic reality that services provide: these exercises can be done at home with a prayer book and gramophone records of sacred music. Rather it must come from satisfactions derived from actual association with other people. What these are, is not known with certainty; it is, however, well established that the presence of other people tends to have an arousing and enlivening effect. It also seems clear that action in unison, such as is involved in the singing of congregational hymns, produces a high ratio of effect to effort, in that each individual feels as if he is in a sense producing the whole result himself.

Whatever the satisfaction that comes from association with others, it is clearly not enough in itself to ensure that church services are attended. For this, a number of aesthetic matters such as beauty of language and music, freedom from distraction, interesting sermons and patent sincerity on the part of clergy are important, and deserve much more attention than they are often given by those responsible for conducting services. Even a number of mundane considerations such as the design, acoustics, heating and lighting of church buildings can be significant. From what we have said about rewards and costs in motivation, we should expect all these various factors to be additive; high quality in any of these respects will enhance, and poor quality detract from, the overall incentive value of the service.

The satisfaction gained from attendance at church services does not depend on any direct interaction between those attending, although it is often believed that satisfaction is enhanced if such interaction occurs. Thus some churches lay stress upon a friendly welcome from sidesmen, a handshake from the minister at the end of a service, or a parish breakfast afterwards, and church services may be supplemented by a range of clubs and societies. The extent to which social contacts are desired, varies between individuals. Some people obtain their main satisfaction from dealings with other people, talking to and influencing them, and receiving replies and influence from them. Others prefer to deal with material things, and take satisfaction in operating machines, driving cars, making various articles and doing odd jobs. Most people show both tendencies to some extent. There are several possible reasons for these tendencies, of which two are especially likely to be important. First, people vary in their normal level of arousal. Those whose normal level is low tend to seek stimulation, and for them social contacts are enlivening and enjoyable. For those whose normal level is high, however, social contacts are unduly stimulating and may make them feel tense and irritable, so that they tend to shun society and to seek quiet (see Welford, 1968, chapter 10). Second, tendencies towards people or things may reflect skills built up in childhood. A child who has been surrounded by people who make demands on him, and take demands from him, will have built up social skills for dealing with these contacts. On the other hand, a child brought up with little human contact will usually have had to turn to toys or other inanimate objects for interest, and will have acquired skills relating to these. Subsequent situations will tend to be met in terms of the skills already formed, so that the tendencies towards people or towards things will be self-perpetuating.

There seems to be one important complication to this relatively simple picture. Some people whose social skill is poor, are nevertheless anxious for social contacts. A possible reason for their being in this position, is that people around them in childhood provided human contact, without making the demands on them which are required to develop social skills fully. They had thus been led to expect too high a ratio of result to effort in their human relationships—in short they had been spoilt. An alternative possibility is that their human contacts were both rewarding and punishing: if, for instance, their mother had been unpredictable, sometimes rewarding and sometimes punishing the same behaviour, the child would have experienced some satisfying human relationships, but have had no means of learning skills to ensure them.

Insofar as people differ in their desires for social contact, churches should clearly make a variety of provisions. People with well developed social skills and needs, will enjoy membership of a church group which engages in a variety of communal activities; and which may perhaps be able to contain and train, by a mixture of kindness and firm frankness, some of those who desire contacts but lack social skills. For those whose social interests are not dominant, attempts to create a warm, friendly atmosphere by such means as cheery greetings at the church door, may be so distasteful that they stay away. For them there may, however, be opportunities they will willingly accept for membership in a manner involving less direct human contact.

One further point about the benefits of group membership

should be noted. The effectiveness of a group and its degree of coherence, are usually enhanced if it has before it an easily understood aim to which all the members can subscribe, and it is often suggested that the Church could be more effective if its aims were stated more clearly. However, one of the striking characteristics of the congregations of the larger denominations is the wide variety of people they contain. Almost certainly, therefore, any formulated aim which was not so general as to be virtually meaningless, would be regarded by some as over-complex and by others as naive, by some as too broad and by others as too narrow, and so on. A precisely stated aim in such a case, would be more divisive than unifying. What is more, the satisfactions gained from church membership in the larger denominations vary widely. Within any one congregation one could, if one looked closely, uncover a delicate and complex network of aims, hopes, satisfactions and benefits, which any undue attempt at uniformity could easily destroy.

Group possessions

Not only common aims, interests and ideals, but also things such as buildings, badges, uniforms, codes of behaviour, ceremonial rituals and books of rules shared by members of a group, tend to foster group coherence. All these are found in various church groups, but obviously the Church's most important group possessions are the Bible and traditional forms of service. There are two points of controversy about these on which psychological comment is pertinent: the authority of the Bible, and the language in which it and church services are expressed.

The argument about what status should be accorded to the Bible is well known. Is it a detailed book of precise rules, or is it a more general guide? Are its indications immutable, or are they subject to reinterpretation as knowledge advances? Are all parts equally important, or do some have greater significance than others? We have seen in the last chapter that those who answer "yes" to the first alternative in each of these questions tend on average to be of relatively simple mind and limited education. This is understandable, since it is intellectually easier to think of the Bible as a book of precise, immutable rules all of which are equally binding, than to regard it as a source of general inspiration and guidance, in which strands of differing importance have to be distinguished, and the interpretation of which may change as new knowledge comes to light. Yet it is clear that the effort must be made to treat the Bible in this latter way, for at least three reasons. First, the authority of the Bible cannot rest on its own statements, but only on the extent to which it proves an effective means of bringing coherence to experience, and yielding guidance towards a life in line with what we have called basic reality. Second, as we noted in Chapter III, the text of the Bible as we now have it, is largely based on oral traditions which were passed from person to person for many years before they were written down, and have suffered the same kinds of simplifications, distortions and additions that have been repeatedly shown to occur in studies of memory. Third, interpretation has undoubtedly changed with increased insight over the years, though usually by way of clarification, rather than by direct negation of what was held previously. Thus many Old Testament stories have been shorn of their supposed historical foundations, but the lessons they conveyed remain: for example, the book of Job is no longer regarded as history, but its treatment of the problem of suffering is in no way affected. The "literal truth" of the Bible believed in by so-called "fundamentalists", is in fact an interpretation which is often a long way from what the original writers meant, and is usually based on a particular translation, rather than on the best available version of the original text.

As regards the language of the Bible and church services, there seems to be a widespread tendency for the authoritative writings of all religions to be expressed in language which is to some extent archaic. The seventeenth-century language of the Church of England Prayer Book and of the Authorised Version of the English Bible are not, therefore, alone in this respect. To some extent, this archaism could be due to their authoritative nature making any change a matter of controversy, which would be regarded as impairing the stability and coherence of the Church. This does not, however, appear to be the whole reason. When, as a result of changes in language over the years, the text of the Authorised Version of the Bible came to be difficult for many people to understand, new translations into modern prose were not universally welcomed, and were accepted with reservations and misgivings. In part, these may have come from a straightforward liking for what is familiar, especially for what has been so from early childhood, but other factors also seem to be important.

The writer once tried an experiment with pairs of prose passages, one in sixteenth or seventeenth-century language, and the other a modern translation of it. Subjects were asked to say which version of each pair they preferred, and why (Welford, 1948). The passages ranged from well-known biblical quotations through less well-known biblical quotations, and non-biblical passages of a religious nature, to secular passages on more mundane topics. Some three-quarters of the subjects, clergy, churchgoers and non-churchgoers equally, preferred the traditional language for the well-known biblical passages, the proportion falling progressively through the less well-known and non-biblical to the secular material. The fall was greater among the clergy and churchgoers than among the non-church-goers: liking of archaic language was much more sharply focused on biblical material among the former than among the latter.

The passages had been chosen and translated in such a way that the archaic language was always of higher literary quality, but less clear in its meaning, than its modern equivalent. Understandably, therefore, most of the reasons given for preference were in terms of "beauty" as opposed to "clarity". Many subjects, however, emphasised the "fittingness" or "appropriateness" of the biblical language for religious matters and of modern language for secular ones. These tendencies appeared to be over and above any influence of sheer familiarity, although this also played a part: archaic language was chosen for about two-thirds of the biblical passages recognised as familiar, but for only about half of those which were unfamiliar.

Somewhat similar preferences for archaic language were found also for prayers (Welford, 1946). Subjects were presented with four prayers, two traditional and two new, with one of each pair in very much simpler, more direct language than the other. Subjects were asked to rank the four prayers in order of preference, and to state their reasons for the order. Those who regarded themselves as churchgoers and, even more, those who were clergy or ordinands, tended to prefer the traditional prayers to the new, and among the latter, the one in traditional language to the simpler prayer. These preferences were reversed among non-churchgoers. The trends were largely independent of age, although somewhat greater preference for simplicity was shown among those under twenty-five, than among those who were older. Two churchgoing groups ran counter to the general trend in preferring the simpler prayers. One, not unexpectedly, was a group of Quakers; the other consisted of churchgoers engaged in work with children as school or Sunday-school teachers or youth leaders. Their liking for simplicity seems to have been due to their identifying with the children they worked with, and was similar to that of children attending church or Sunday school. Surprisingly, children who attended neither of these organisations made somewhat more traditional choices, for example, of the two new prayers, they preferred the one in traditional language.

The reasons given for preferences made it very clear that, as one went from non-churchgoers, through lay-churchgoers to clergy and ordinands, concern with the ideas expressed in the prayers, and desire for simplicity, gave way to interest in more aesthetic features such as "beauty" and "dignity" of expression, and that these features were more important than sheer familiarity. This finding seems to be in line with other aspects of church services in many denominations. For example, in the case of hymns and anthems, most people who go to church probably derive more from the music than from the words, and the vividly emotional preacher usually makes a greater immediate impact than one who is less spectacular. It is perhaps fair to argue that the seeming indifference of church-goers to the rational content of prayers, hymns and biblical readings is more apparent than real—familiarity enables church-goers to recognise meaningful content well enough for them to give their main attention to aesthetic aspects, whereas non-churchgoers cannot appreciate the beauty of language and music, because they are having to struggle to understand the ideas being conveyed.

The price of change

The results of these experiments suggest that certain changes such as the 1967 revision of the Church of England Communion Service, the substitution of the vernacular for Latin in the Roman Mass, and the language of the New English Bible, were not as well conceived as they might at first sight appear to have been. All these changes were designed to make the language simpler and more readily understandable, and in this they have been largely successful. Yet in achieving clarity, the beauty of the original Latin or of the seventeenth-century English has been destroyed, and with it many familiar and cherished expressions. The somewhat cynical assumption appears to have been that the increased clarity of the Bible and church services, will make them appeal to people who would not be interested in them in their traditional forms, and that recruitment to the Church from among these people will more than offset any losses suffered by those who prefer what has been replaced. We may question this assumption in two ways: first, are beauty and clarity necessarily incompatible; and second, will the increased clarity of the new versions really make Christianity available to people who are now outside it?

One method of achieving both beauty and clarity would be to arrange for both old and new forms of service to be held on different occasions, at least while members of present congregations survive. This solution is obviously possible in large centres of population, but would probably be difficult to achieve in rural areas. The alternative is to make further revisions aimed at achieving the literary quality of the Authorised Version of the Bible and the Church of England Prayer Book in forms fully understandable to modern ears. This appears to be the more promising solution, since if our results are correct, sheer familiarity is less important for present churchgoers than aesthetic quality. If quality of expression was achieved along with clarity, they would probably come to accept new forms fairly quickly.

The more serious problem is whether the clarity aimed at in the new versions of the Bible and services is likely to be of help to those who do not at present understand Christianity. The remarks made by the subjects of our experiments who chose simplicity, implied that they were seeking clarity of *ideas* rather than of language, and that what they found difficult in the traditional forms was not the occasional archaic word or expression, but Christian terms such as "grace" or "salvation" or what is meant by eating the body and drinking the blood of Christ. It is obviously too much to suggest that the meanings of these terms should be spelt out every time they now appear in the Bible or Prayer Book. A more practical approach would be to institute a teaching campaign accompanied, perhaps, by carefully prepared manuals, setting out the meanings of these terms in the same way that the meanings of scientific terms are set out in technical glossaries. Such a campaign would, however, almost certainly involve far more than teaching the definitions of a few words. Rather we should find it necessary to overhaul our whole manner of expressing Christian doctrine, and undertake a major task of integrating it with modern secular knowledge. Yet it is this kind of clarification that is really needed. This being so, any new version of the Bible or Prayer Book which merely substitutes modern idiom and vocabulary, without any more radical retranslation of ideas, fails doubly. On the one hand, by destroying familiar beauty, it does violence to those for whom traditional forms are valuable parts of their Christian heritage; while on the other hand, by failing to make Christian ideas understandable, it is unlikely to have any impact beyond present church members.

DIVERSITY AND UNITY

The present divisions of the Church are largely due to accidents of history. Various denominations split off from others because of local circumstances during a particular period of time, or because new insights grew faster than existing denominations were able to absorb them. Perpetuation of these divisions seems to be due, in large part, to the fact that people tend to prefer the style of worship which was made familiar to them in childhood. However, there is a considerable body of evidence that those who belong to different denominations, differ in a number of significant ways (for a summary see Argyle, 1958, chapter 8). For example, in Britain members of the Church of England tend to vote Conservative more than Nonconformists, Roman Catholics or those with no religious affiliation. In the U.S.A., more Protestants than Roman Catholics tend to vote Republican; Episcopalians tend to earn more, and to be of higher occupational status than other Protestants, and these are in turn higher than Roman Catholics. Similar average differences between denominations are found for intelligence test scores. As regards personality, average differences as measured by tests of extraversion-introversion and stability of temperament are small (Brown, 1969), but Roman Catholics tend to be more authoritarian in outlook than members of most Protestant denominations and, in the U.S.A., less tolerant of negroes and Jews. They are also less inclined to commit suicide, perhaps because they are more inclined to direct the aggressive tendencies which may occur in frustrating conditions towards other people rather than themselves (Brown, 1965). Types of crime committed also tend to vary between members of different denominations: Roman Catholics incline more to crimes of violence, and Protestants to sexual offences. Regular churchgoers, whether or not they are nominally members of a church, have lower crime rates than non-churchgoers.

The reasons for these differences are not clear, and the methods employed in some of the studies have been questioned (Nowlan, 1957), although the main trends seem to be well enough established. It is probably significant that denomination, at least in Britain and the U.S.A., tends to go with national and racial origin. Thus, Roman Catholics in these countries are predominantly Irish, Italian or Polish in origin, whereas Protestants are predominantly English, Scottish, Welsh, German or Scandinavian. Whatever the reasons for denominational differences, however, it is clear that present denominations minister to groups of people who differ appreciably in a number of ways, and are likely to have different interests, outlooks, problems and needs.

It must be emphasised that we are speaking of average trends. There is a great deal of overlap between denominations, so that many members of one will have characteristics more typical of another, and vice versa. How far the differences between the services and other activities of the various denominations can be attributed to the average differences between their members, has never, to the present writer's knowledge, been examined in detail. We have, however, seen in previous chapters that members of extreme Protestant sects which emphasise the rewarding of the faithful and the punishment of others in an after life, tend to live under various economic and self-imposed stresses, for which their beliefs can be regarded as a form of compensation.

Church Union

If what was said earlier in this chapter about the benefits of group membership is true, present denominations are likely to unite if, but only if, it will enable them to do their work for individual members better than if they remain distinct. One obvious benefit would be economic: a united Church could make substantial savings on buildings, organisation and personnel. Another advantage would be the strength that unity would bring to meeting secular attacks. We may note, in these connections, that current moves towards church reunion, coincide with a period of serious financial difficulty for almost all denominations, and of political or social attack in several countries.

Thoroughgoing union which resulted in all denominational differences being abolished would, however, have several disadvantages. There would be certain temporary difficulties due to the fact that, if the full benefits of union were to be obtained, congregations would have to be combined. This would involve loss of familiar practices, forms of service, buildings, and other group possessions, on which some of the stability of religion seems to depend, especially for older people. There would also be some difficult problems of redundancy among both ministers and laymen when combining the organisations concerned. These difficulties could be overcome in time with careful arrangements and tact. Certain other disadvantages would, however, be inevitable and continuing. The most serious and fundamental of these is that denominational differences are, almost certainly, an important means of matching the ministrations of the Church to the needs of different sections of the population: uniformity of services and other activities would mean that many individuals would be less well catered for than they are now. Also, the fact that congregations would have to be fewer and larger if the economic benefits of union were to be achieved, would mean that the enthusiasm, team spirit and local pride found in many small congregations would be lost (Wicker, 1969), and problems of leadership might be increased.

The basic limitation of leadership, which sets a maximum to the number of people that can be effectively led, appears to lie in the fact that processing of incoming data and of decisions about action, takes time, so that there is a maximum of data and decision that one person can effectively handle. Put another way, time is required to resolve uncertainty about which of several possible events has occurred, and which of various possible actions needs to be taken. There is thus a maximum amount of uncertainty that an individual can resolve in any given time. The individual members of a group generate, for a leader, an amount of uncertainty which depends upon the nature of the activity they are engaged in, the conditions under which it is done, and their personal characteristics. The size of group that one person can lead effectively depends on the total uncertainty from all these sources. Thus, a group can be large if it is engaged in a routine activity under stable conditions, and its members are of even temperament; but it must be smaller if the activities or the conditions are variable, or if there are un-stable personalities among the group. Any complete union between denominations would tend not only to enlarge congregations, but to increase the variety of people comprising them, and probably also the range of problems with which a parish minister would have to deal. The total increase could well take the task of leadership beyond the powers of one man.

Even the rivalry between denominations, which is regarded as one of the most damaging scandals of the present-day church, is not entirely to be deplored. A moderate degree of rivalry between groups encourages coherence and effort. While it is unworthy to take pride in having a larger congregation or collection, or a more active Sunday-school than a neighbouring parish, the effort resulting from competition may spill over to the more fundamental aims of Christianity and if it does, there will be some truth in the remark that the more religious a nation is, the more divided is its church.

The problems we have outlined would not apply to a union between denominations in the sense of mutual respect and recognition, and of co-operation in scholarship, research, teaching, and social action. Such a union would preserve the subtlety and variety of what the Church provides in its present denominations, but would reduce the division of society and wasteful use of resources, of which the denominations are at present accused.

One further warning needs to be sounded, although an unpopular one in the present climate of opinion. It is that changes should be made with caution. Any industrial consultant will agree that, when he goes into a factory which uses well-established practices, he can find some points at which change could make work more efficient or less stressful, but that overall efficiency is usually high. Over the years the frequent, small insights of those on the job and those managing it, have produced a series of minor changes which have steadily improved the method of work, and brought it to a high pitch of efficiency. Most of these changes have been made without those concerned fully realising how well they were doing, and those on the job at any time seldom recognise just which features of their procedure are good, and which are in need of change. Often some of those regarded as essential are in fact unnecessary, and change of some which are regarded as unsatisfactory would, in fact, make matters worse. So it must often be in other human organisations, including the Church. Many seemingly unimportant activities, probably play a crucial part in the lives of many church members, so that serious losses would ensue if the activities were changed. At the same time, features of church life which most people regard as vital, could probably be dropped with little if any untoward result. In short, proposals for change in the Church should be based on a substantial programme of research into their possible effects. It is fair to claim that the Church and its activities merit at least as careful research as is demanded before a new drug or aircraft is put into use.

Chapter VI

Human Relations

THE description of man as a servo-mechanism, which we have touched on in Chapters I and IV, emphasises that human behaviour is not a series of simple responses to stimuli, but consists of continuously developing patterns in which each action depends, in broad outline, on some overall aim, and in detail upon the outcome of previous actions. Thus the driver of a car observes the road situation and his car's position in it and manipulates the controls, the car responds and changes position, the driver observes again, and so on: the process of observation, action, feedback of data about the results of action, and taking of fresh action, goes on continuously.

The same description in servo-mechanism terms can be applied to human beings interacting with each other (Welford 1966, 1968 chapter 10). One person speaks, or performs an action, and the other perceives, interprets and responds. The first perceives, interprets and responds to the other's response, and so on. How well their exchange of information goes, will depend on how accurately each is able to interpret what the other says and does, and how far each is able to make an adequate response to, and elicit a reaction from, the other. Thus if both speak the same language, are interested in the same things and are polite and encouraging to each other, conversation is likely to flow freely. If, however, one speaks English and the other Chinese, or if they have no common interests, or if one is abrupt or aloof with the other, conversation will quickly cease.

These simple, and indeed obvious, principles provide a powerful aid to clear thinking about human relations, and in this chapter we shall discuss certain important examples in these terms. We shall look first at the nature of *friendship* and *enmity*, definition of which has proved remarkably elusive in the past. We shall then go on to examine certain other relationships, first within the family, then outside. Finally we shall attempt to sum up, by considering what is meant by Christian *love*.

FRIENDSHIP AND ENMITY

Let us consider first the case of casual friendly acquaintance at a party, where conversation flows between two people with growing mutual approval. Four things seem to be characteristic of this situation. First, each speaker obviously understands what the other is saying, not only in the sense that they talk the same language, but that they code or conceive of objects and events in ways which they both comprehend. Second, the two speakers are roughly matched in the pace at which they produce their ideas, so that neither overloads the other by going too fast, nor bores him by going too slowly. Third, each is able and willing to adapt his remarks to the other, in the sense of modifying his statements and behaviour in the light of the replies and behaviour of the other — in short, each is sensitive to feedback from the other. Fourth, each, in the ideas he produces, supplements or complements those of the other. Although they may not always agree, each obtains a set of ideas larger than he could produce alone, and is thus able to think more easily, more constructively or with greater satisfaction than he could on his own. Both thus stimulate each other: in engineering terms, the feedback between them is positive. This may not always be so in more mature friendships, where a person may sometimes speak or act to criticise or discourage his friend. In such cases, however, the restraint seems to be a temporary phase within a larger, long-term framework of mutual encouragement and facilitation.

Enmity or hostility seems to involve processes which are, broadly speaking, the reverse of those found in friendship. Conversation and other activities such as fighting between enemies, may produce temporary exchanges in which each reacts to the other and observes the other's reactions, thus securing a feedback situation. Sophisticated forms of hostility may include simulated friendship, with spells in which each leads the other on to greater and greater response. However, the long-term aim of one or both parties in all cases, is to reduce the other to a state in which he is unable to act or retires from the scene, so that feedback ceases.

While, therefore, friendship is fundamentally constructive and expansive, enmity is essentially destructive. It is true that the rivalry that enmity produces can be stimulating, so that just as scientific advances may come more rapidly in war than in peacetime, individual enemies may spur each other to achievements they would never otherwise have attained. In such cases, however, extra achievement is usually offset to an appreciable extent, by waste of effort and loss of time incurred by one or both parties in trying to undo each other's work, and by losses to third parties who may have been directly or indirectly affected. Enmity is thus always inefficient. One of the outstanding problems of human relationships is to secure the stimulating effects of rivalry within an overall framework of friendship: in other words, to compete in achievement without at the same time seeking to lower the achievement of others.

CHRISTIANITY: A PSYCHOLOGIST'S TRANSLATION

Let us try to apply the principles we have used to define friendship, to certain of the close personal relationships found between husband and wife, and between parents and children.

Marriage and sex

The preface to the marriage service in the Church of England Prayer Book lists three "causes for which Matrimony was ordained": first, for the procreation of children to be brought up as Christians; second, for the regulation of sexual intercourse; and third, for companionship between man and woman – "for the mutual society, help and comfort that the one ought to have of the other, both in prosperity and adversity." It is, perhaps, an indication that our sensitivities have advanced since the seventeenth century that these three causes now appear to be in the wrong order. The first essential of a really contented marriage would appear to be friendship, so that each partner is in some sense a "bigger" person, more at peace with himself and the world than he would otherwise be. The continual intimacy of marriage is an exacting relationship: husband and wife cannot get away from each other in times of difficulty to the same extent as ordinary friends, so that unless there is a profound and thorough friendship between them, they will grate on each other and quarrel. The attempt to prevent this happening will mean trying to prevent feedback from each other and will thus turn them into enemies.

The deep friendship required in marriage does not demand identity of interests, but it does mean a complementary and mutually encouraging relationship; and this, in turn, implies that partners need to choose each other with care. Many men and women could make marriages of sorts together, but unless they have taken trouble when finding each other, or have been exceptionally lucky, their relationships are likely to lack the easy two-way traffic of thought, help and companionship that make a marriage satisfying.

All this is not to say that other aspects of marriage are unimportant. Freud (1916) tells how, as a postgraduate medical student in Paris, he heard Charcot, the most striking neuropsychiatrist of the day, declare that hysterical symptoms always originated from something wrong with the patient's sex life. Subsequent study has confirmed that a great deal of minor mental ill-health, which can make people miserable and sour their relationships with those around them, are indeed associated with failure to find the contentment that can come from sexual union in marriage. Which, however, is cause and which is effect, is less easy to say. Some marital disharmony may indeed be due to lack of understanding, or to prejudice or ineptitude on the part of husband or wife, and be curable by suitable instruction; but one suspects that, usually, lack of sexual harmony derives from the fact that the essential friendship and companionship of marriage are not there. It is often suggested that the profound pleasure of sexual union between two people who feel deeply and fully for each other, is symbolic of their love – that is of the ready and satisfying two-way relationship that exists between them. If so, it is perhaps fair to argue that the feelings engendered by sexual union are always symbolic of the relationships between the partners. For example, sex for kicks or for relieving tension, betokens a selfish attitude in which there is no real two-way relationship, because each partner is interested only in his or her own pleasure. By the same tokens, people who are married in law but lack the friendship to make their marriage companionable, are likely to find their lack of feeling for each other reflected in an unsatisfying sex life.

Much the same should probably be said of sexual relationships by married people outside their marriage. Such relationships are likely to hurt and alienate the other partner of the marriage, to destroy their confidence in having someone to whom they are uniquely valuable, and to undermine the stability of the home – all consequences which would not be contemplated if the friendship appropriate to marriage existed. Indeed, if there is genuine companionship between husband and wife, intercourse with other people will seem revolting.

What about sexual intercourse before marriage? The issues regarding this today are different from those of any previous generation. Efficient contraception has greatly reduced the danger of unwanted pregnancies, which was formerly the most powerful argument against pre-marital intercourse: instead it is argued that sexual experience is educative, aiding the attainment of emotional maturity, and of technique to be used later in marriage. The main argument today against intercourse before marriage, is that it can produce results which are damaging to emotional stability. On the one hand, it can intensify an emotional attachment between a man and a woman who are seriously interested in the possibility of marriage, but who do not know each other well enough to be sure they have the necessary basis for a lasting companionship. If, as they come to know each other better, one or other of them decides to break off, the parting will be the more painful, and can have seriously unsettling effects: for example, many students have had their university careers wrecked by being unable to concentrate on their studies after the breaking of an intensely emotional engagement. On the other hand, easy sex without deep feeling, is liable to cheapen sexual intercourse into a routine pleasure with no special significance. When this happens, motivation can be distorted, since other pleasures may become tame after the intense sensual satisfaction of sex, and the chance of making intercourse the unique symbol of deeply-felt friendship and affection has been lost.

At present, we do not know for certain how valid these arguments are, either for or against sex before marriage. We are, however, living through a time when many young men and women are unwittingly carrying out a large-scale experiment, using themselves as subjects. It remains for the future to assess what results, for good or evil, the freer sexual behaviour of the last few years may produce.

Sex cannot generate the friendship needed for marriage, but it can set a seal upon it. The same is true of children. When they are desired and valued by both husband and wife, children can strengthen the companionship their parents already possess. Children are, however, unlikely to produce companionship in a marriage where it is absent. The suggestion is sometimes made to a married couple who are unhappy with each other, that they should have a child to "strengthen their marriage". Since upbringing in an unharmonious home can be damaging to a child's development, it is surely irresponsible – indeed wicked – advice to propose that life be forced on a child in order to sustain its parents' marriage; and heeding such advice is one of the most reprehensible actions a man and woman can take.

Almost equally reprehensible is the action of a husband or wife who insists on having a child, against the wishes of the other. Essentially this means that the one partner has used the other as a tool for his or her own purposes, and the child will tend to weaken the friendship between them instead of symbolising and strengthening it. The partner desiring a child in this way is usually the wife, who is compelled by a strong instinctive urge first to bear, and then to possess, children. The results can be serious: many a woman neglects her husband once he has given her the children she wants, and in later life can push her children into unsuitable marriages in the hope of obtaining grandchildren. In either case she is tending to destroy the stability of the home, which is important for the sound up-bringing of the very children or grandchildren concerned. The blind force of "the flesh" in the form of maternal instinct is one of the human characteristics most in need of better understand-ing today, and on which the Church's attitudes seem to require careful reappraisal.

Parent and child

Understanding and feedback, which are the essentials of friend-ship, are also of importance in the relations between children and their parents. We have already mentioned that a child needs stability at home. A situation in which the results of actions are predictable, makes it easier to learn the skills needed for dealing with day to day problems, and avoids the risk of stress, due to sudden events which the child does not know how to handle. In short, stability means that a child can the more easily get to know the "coding" of his world, and discover how to make his way about in it. Loss of such stability is probably, from the child's point of view, the most serious consequence of his parents becoming divorced. The anxiety that results can seriously disrupt education and the development of personality, and is probably the most powerful present-day argument against divorce. The damaging effects are not confined to young children, but seem often to be at least as serious, if not more so, in the teens and during early adulthood. Indeed it can be fairly argued that a husband and wife should not have a child unless they can see their way to living harmoniously together, at least until the child is about twenty-five years old. The same kind of danger, although less serious, comes from frequent changes of school, as when father takes a series of jobs in different places over a relatively short period of years.

The importance of feedback is indicated by the repeated emphasis laid, in studies of upbringing, on the need for mother and child to have a "warm, accepting relationship", and by the difficulties that may ensue if mother goes out to work, and is thus not at home to greet her child when it returns from school. Feedback appears to operate in at least three ways.

First, if a child obtains understandable answers to questions, the interpretation of events, especially unknown events, is made easier and he is rapidly reassured against the anxieties and fears that may come from the unknown.

Second, and at least equally important, a child needs guidance if it is to develop its skills quickly and fully. This is especially true during the early years. Skills are cumulative, in the sense that we inevitably deal with any new situation in terms we have brought to it from other situations in the past. First impressions, such as those of early childhood are thus especially important. Many recent psychological studies have confirmed the fact, long known to instructors in typewriting and various games and sports, that if a trainee learns an incorrect technique in the early stages, the fault may be very difficult to correct later. These studies have also emphasised, however, that if a trainee is to learn quickly and to retain what he has learnt, he needs to discover for himself how to deal with his task. The instructor is thus faced with a difficult dual requirement: his training methods must ensure that the trainee not only makes active decisions about what to do, instead of being merely shown, but at the same time always makes these decisions correctly (for a brief review see Welford, 1968, chapter 9). Similar principles apply to children, and require a delicate balance between freedom to experiment, instruction and correction. The right balance seems more likely to be achieved if parents and teachers join in their children's activities, and so ensure a full two-way traffic between the children and themselves, than if children learn simply by watching films or television. With these, the traffic is entirely one-way, since the viewer has no influence on the sequence of events presented on the screen, and thus no need to decide upon action or to check whether he has understood what has been presented.

Third, and perhaps most important, if a child is to be able to pursue long-term purposes, and to co-operate in group situations, it must not only have freedom to develop its capacities and to explore its world, but must also acquire self-discipline to control its immediate whims and desires, and to avoid being a nuisance to others. For this purpose, two principles clearly emerge from psychological studies of both human beings and animals. One is that a child, like a laboratory animal, will quickly learn to do what in some way or other "pays". This does not mean that it needs continual money or other rewards for being "good", but rather that any behaviour which secures what it regards as a favourable outcome, will tend to be repeated. Thus, for example, a child who finds that if it whines in temper when mother says "No", she will eventually relent and say "Yes", will always whine when it is frustrated, because it has learnt that this is a means of getting its own way. Experimental studies have shown, as we noted in Chapter II, that the lesson will be learnt even if success is not always achieved—behaviour may, indeed, be more persistent if it is only occasionally rewarded. If it is to be eliminated, it must never in any circumstances be successful.

The other principle is that some feedback, in the form of reward, punishment or both, is necessary. There has been considerable controversy about the relative merits of these, and especially about the value of punishment, following the reaction of many psychological theorists during the early years of the century, away from Victorian severity. It was argued that anything tending to restrict or frustrate a child's desires is likely to impair its mental development and increase the likelihood of neurotic disturbance in later life. More recently, it has come to be recognised that lack of adequate discipline can also have serious consequences. For example, several studies have suggested that permissiveness by parents leads to aggressive tendencies in children, both immediately and at later ages (Sears *et al.* 1957, McCord *et al.* 1962, Weatherley, 1962, Sollenberger, 1968, Goldstein *et al.* 1970). The issues are clearer if punishment is not viewed as a retribution for wrongdoing, or a means of making a child frightened to do what it should not, but if both reward and punishment are thought of as having two essential functions: first of making right action "pay", and second of conveying information about which actions are right, and which wrong.

As regards the first of these two functions, it is important to consider rewards and punishments in relation to individual desires, interests and personality: what is rewarding to one person may be neutral or even punishing to another; what is a mild punishment to one person may be severe to another. As regards the second function, it is important to recognise that reward and punishment may not convey the same information. If, for example, a choice has to be made between several lines of action, only one of which is correct, reward for taking this line will convey more precise information than punishment for taking another line: reward will indicate exactly which line is right, whereas punishment will indicate merely that one of several possible wrong lines of action has been taken, leaving the subject in doubt about which of the others is right. If there are only two alternatives, reward and punishment should have equal indicating effects, although these are suggestions that even in this case, reward is a little better: we seem able to accept positive indications that one alternative is right, more easily than indirect indications that one is right because another is wrong.

Broadly speaking, we should expect that rewards and punishments as conveyors of information, should be effective even if relatively mild. This appears to be true in the sense that, as we noted in Chapter IV, the giving and withdrawing of affection are often more effective than lavish rewards or severe corporal punishment. Children seem able to adapt to corporal punishment: for example a boy who is smacked at home, or caned at school, regularly for minor offences, comes to accept this treatment as an inescapable hazard of life, rather than an indicator of what should or should not be done. This does not mean to say that generous rewards or a sharp smack should never be given, and indeed there are indications that those brought up with direct physical punishments, tend to be less likely to need psychiatric care than those whose punishment has been the withdrawal of parents' love — the conscience built up by withdrawal of love may become too active, and lead to excessive guilt feelings and depression (Greenfield, 1959). The overall implication is the obvious one, that some grading of rewards and punishments is required, to distinguish not only between right and wrong, but between different degrees of each.

One further point about over-generous rewards and over-severe punishments needs to be mentioned. Experimental studies have shown that, while mild rewards and punishments stimulate a subject to better performance than he would otherwise attain, a high level of reward may produce over-excitement and a high level of punishment may lead to disabling fear. Either type of disturbance tends to disrupt learning and performance, especially of more difficult tasks, and among more highly-strung subjects (for a brief review, see Welford, 1968, chapters 8 and 10). It is important to recognise that the levels of praise and blame, or other rewards and punishments, which will bring out the best efforts of a happy-go-lucky, cheerfully irresponsible person, can be seriously disturbing to one who is more sensitive and conscientious. Failure of parents, and of school and university teachers to recognise this fact, must lead every year to a great deal of wasted talent, either from failure to stimulate insensitive children and students or, more often, from pushing sensitive ones too hard, making them chronically anxious and unable to concentrate on high-grade intellectual work (Welford, 1965).

The Church is involved in these matters, not only because of its traditional concern with family life, but because those sects which emphasise the view that man is inevitably worthless and sinful, and that his only hope of salvation lies in intense and unremitting effort, can reinforce tendencies by parents and teachers to stress some children and adolescents too severely. Anyone who has had a close concern for the welfare of under-graduates, will have seen the damage that can sometimes be done by an extreme evangelical sect to a highly-strung, hard-working student. On the other hand, he will also have observed the support, comfort and relief that such a student can obtain from less austere forms of Christianity.

The elderly

For many people as they grow older, there comes a time when they have to rely on those younger for help. At first, this may only be for occasional advice and assistance at times of special difficulty. Later, more and more everyday support is sought, until the stage is reached of complete and continuous nursing care. While husband and wife are both living, they usually support each other in these ways. Problems arise, however, when one partner dies and the other, usually the woman, since women tend to live longer than men, seeks help from the next generation. The source of help preferred by most elderly people is a daughter or son, and this is understandable since they will be familiar with ways of thought and speech, likes and dislikes, that have become familiar within the family, and make two-way exchanges between members of the family relatively easy. We shall here for convenience speak only about mother and daughter, because this is the most frequent relationship concerned; but most of what we have to say applies equally to other relationships between the elderly and the middle-aged.

Townsend (1957) in a study of old people in the east end of London, gives evidence which indicates that a daughter can assume a substantial measure of responsibility for her ageing mother without great difficulty, so long as the care required and contact with her mother are intermittent, and there is some reciprocal help – for example, so long as "granny" can be of genuine help with the daughter's young children. Difficulty arises, however, when contact is maintained continuously as, for example, when the mother comes to live with the daughter and her husband in their home, or when the mother requires care but is unable or unwilling to give any useful help in return. Essentially, difficulty seems to occur when the necessary conditions of friendship between members of the family break down. Often this is because mother fails to take sufficient account of her daughter's wishes, and promotes only her own. She attempts to maintain the achievement of earlier years by supplementing her own efforts with those of her daughter, so that she becomes demanding. Many parents, indeed, plan for this demand, and argue that one of the advantages of having children is that they can "look after you when you are old." The children have, of course, had no opportunity of deciding whether or not they are willing to be born on such conditions: they are merely told, in effect, "When you were a child I did everything for you; now you must do everything for me." This attitude seems often to be enhanced by a desire for prestige.

Mother has seen in the working world of her husband and her unmarried women acquaintances, that age tends to bring promotion with widening responsibilities and command of others. She feels that her promotion lies in being the undisputed head of a circle of sons, daughters and grandchildren, and it is a proud moment when she can say: "My daughter never leaves me", or "My grandchildren always come to see me on Sundays."

A more fundamental difficulty for elderly mothers seems to be that the experiences of pregnancy, giving birth, and the early days of motherhood are, at least in retrospect, so pleasurable that no subsequent events can ever match up to them. As a result, the elderly mother is chronically discontented, and seeks to reinstate her early years by thinking of her middle-aged children as still young, and therefore to be organised and disciplined; and of her grandchildren as babies to be petted and indulged. She thus loads her children with advice, and spoils her grandchildren. Her advice is unwelcome, not only because it is unsought, but because the very great advances of knowledge in recent years about health, food values and other matters involved in running a home, mean that it is likely to be unsound.

Looking at the problem from the daughter's point of view, the presence of an elderly mother in the house, invades the privacy of husband and wife, and can severely complicate their relationships with their children. This results not only from the factors we have already mentioned, but from the fact that the daughter and son-in-law may be severely overloaded. An elderly mother living in their home may call upon them for help many times during the day and night, so that they are chronically fatigued; and the point can quickly be reached when husband and wife cannot go out together, and family holidays are impossible, because "granny" cannot, or will not, be left alone. The situation is most obviously serious when the elderly mother is chronically ill, but overloading can be appreciable even when she is fit and well: however accommodating she is, her presence and the need to fit another member into the family, will add to the constraints and complications of life for those with whom she lives.

There is a further type of overloading which can seriously disrupt family life, although in a less obvious manner. It derives from the tendency for many older people to talk more and listen less, coupled with the restriction of interests they often display. There are plausible biological reasons for these changes with age: it is usually easier to dictate the course of a conversation by talking, than it is to follow someone else's thoughts when listening; and restriction of interests is a way in which those whose capacities are failing, can maximise achievement by concentrating their efforts on a narrow front. The effect, however, is to load the family with talking which conveys little or no information likely to interest them — the classical conditions for producing boredom.

The way of obviating these difficulties is for old people who are no longer able to look after themselves and require continuous or almost continuous care, to go into a home specially organised for the elderly. Old people are often unwilling to do this, however, believing that they will get more of the attention they want from a daughter or son, than they will from strangers. Their children also are often unwilling for them to go, feeling guilty at not doing their utmost for their parent, and perhaps fearing the self-righteous criticism of neighbours who do not share their burden. In comment on these attitudes, it seems pertinent to make four points:

First, children owe nothing to their parents for having produced them and brought them up. Parents have children either because they actively want them or because of carelessness. In either case they have a duty to provide their children with the best upbringing they can. The children take whatever up-bringing they are given, because they have no alternative, and they incur no debt to their parents for what they receive.

Second, old people may not feel they like having to continue to make efforts in daily living, but there is some evidence that if they do so, they enjoy life more, and are healthier than they would otherwise be (Kleemeier, 1951).

Third, when the task of looking after an old person becomes severe and unremitting, the choice between their being cared for by a married child and going into a special home, is a choice between gratifying the old person's desires and preserving the integrity of the rest of the family. This is not so with an un-married daughter, but in this case the care of an old person can take up the whole of the daughter's life for a period of years, probably preventing her from making a career, and perhaps from being married.

Fourth, a good home for old people can, in a number of ways, provide better care and a more varied and stimulating life, than can possibly be given by a daughter or son. Some old people realise this once they have moved into such a home, and know that by doing so, a more satisfactory relationship with sons and daughters has been preserved, than would have been under any other conditions.

OUTSIDE THE FAMILY

It is obviously impossible here to survey all the types of human relationship met with in daily life. We shall, however, look at three areas which epitomise important types of situation, and which lend themselves to relatively straightforward discussion in the terms we have used for friendship and enmity at the beginning of this chapter.

Employer and employee

If a group is to function well and to maintain its morale and efficiency under changing circumstances, there must be some feedback to the leader from those led. This is true of any organisation, but the principles are probably most explicitly recognised in industry, and it is this situation that we shall consider by way of example. Almost everything that applies there, has relevance also to the Church, and in what follows we could well read "Church" for "industry" throughout.

The employee's channel of communication back to his employer need not have any formal basis, such as that provided by trade unions or works councils. Communication is often easier, faster and more effective if individuals have the opportunity of making suggestions and complaints to an understanding member of management. Trade unions or other representatives may take a great deal of persuading before they are willing to convey an individual's views, and negotiations through them may be distorted by other issues being discussed at the same time. Lack of a formal mechanism for representation of employees' views does not, therefore, mean that none exists, and presence of a formal mechanism does not mean that feedback is effective.

Trouble seems most commonly to arise when the two-way traffic between employer and employee, or between manager and shop-floor worker breaks down. The interests of both parties makes this all too liable to occur, unless the utmost care is taken to prevent it. In any industrial organisation, each side is essential to the other, but each tends to feel that it would be easier if they could gain power, so that they would not have to take the other's wishes into consideration. Clearly, however, if such an aim was fully achieved by management it would lead to oppression, and if it was achieved by shop-floor workers the result would be at best inefficiency, and at worst chaos. Organisation there must be, and this means that someone must give orders for others to obey. The problem is to ensure that there is, at the same time, a route by which responsible criticism can be heard, and new ideas put forward.

For effective two-way communication to occur, there must not only be an opportunity, in the sense of a formal or informal organisation which makes communication possible, but also a set of attitudes that together form what is broadly termed "good will". Prominent among these is an adequate understanding by each side of the other's problems and ways of thinking about them, such as knowledge by management of methods of budgeting in a wage-earner's home, and of the subtle nexus of human relationships and prestige that attaches to a man and his family in virtue of his position at work. There must also be mutual respect for each other's responsibilities and limitations, and above all, a humble willingness to recognise sound argument and to modify one's views when convinced by it. All these attitudes imply that each side must have a genuine regard for the interests of the other, as well as of its own: management needs to be at pains to organise well, so as to give shop-floor workers the opportunity to do their work efficiently and without unnecessary strain; while shop-floor workers need to be concerned to give an honest and conscientious performance.

Similar considerations apply to the relationships between industry and the general public. Industry needs to accept the results of market research and to listen carefully to complaints from retailers and consumers, not merely because it is likely to do better business as a result, but because the essential reason for its existence is to provide a service to the public – an industry run exclusively or primarily for the benefit of those who own, manage or work in it, is parasitic on the world's resources and peoples. So-called public ownership does not avoid this danger — indeed it tends to increase it: the public corporation or government department does not depend on profit for its survival, and thus tends to become insensitive of public desires and reactions. The public inevitably depends upon industry, in that it must use industry's products or go without. If relationships are to be satisfactory, industry should in its turn depend upon the public. Many of the more successful firms have indeed kept this aim before them, and that their attempts to supply sound goods that people want at the right price, have brought high profits and wages. Those familiar with the Bible may be reminded of the statement that if one seeks first the rule and justice of God, the necessities and amenities of life will come automatically (Matthew 6:33).

Welfare

The requirements for effective relationships between employer and employee, apply also to the dispenser and recipient of welfare. Again the key principle is that there should be a two-way relationship, in which each respects the other. For the dispenser, this implies competence to recognise the recipient's true needs, objectivity in deciding how to meet them, a genuine, selfless concern to see them satisfied, and a delicacy to avoid unnecessary trampling upon the sensitivities of those in distress. The condescending attitude sometimes seen, ministers more to the self-esteem of the dispenser than to the needs of the recipient.

This does not mean, however, that the dispenser should have an unquestioning, blind trust in the client. Just as a doctor has to see behind his patient's immediate symptoms to the disease that is causing them, so the welfare worker often cannot take the client's story at face value, but must look behind it to find his real problem. This is not only so when the client is deliberately selecting his facts in order to tell a convincing story, but is often even more so when he is trying to be truthful, but does not understand the root cause of his problem. Thus, for example, a client's inability to pay his rent, may not mean real poverty so much as excessive smoking or drinking, or inability to resist impulses to spend or bet. Again, inability to work may not be due to the physical disabilities of which the client complains, so much as to deficiencies of personality which make him unable to concentrate, or to co-operate with others.

In such cases, it is worse than useless merely to give money. Doing so will only teach the client that spinning a hard-luck story pays, and will thus damage his character rather than build it up. What is needed, is a continuing relationship in which there is a careful and precise diagnosis of his trouble, followed by action which will lead him gradually to the point at which he can stand on his own feet, or at least attain the highest degree of independence of which he is capable. The first move in establishing this relationship has to be taken by the welfare agency giving help generously and freely, once the appropriate action has been identified. Subsequent actions need to depend on the client's attempts to help himself. These may be feeble and hesitant at first, but if the welfare action has been correct, and if response by the client is insisted upon, they should gradually become more positive. The rare cases in which no response is obtained despite the best efforts of an insightful welfare worker, are probably due to an underlying medical disorder, and should be appropriately referred.

Although, therefore, for some, especially those beset by genuine sickness or accident, support from welfare agencies in the form of money is appropriate, support in most cases needs to take other forms. These will include psychiatric help to overcome the feelings of insecurity and social incompetence which seem often to lead to excessive smoking and drinking, sheltered work where those with mental impairments can use what powers they have without the risk of being exploited by either employers or workmates, and, especially for women, help with household budgeting and guidance in caring for children. A religious welfare organisation can add a further provision which is beyond the scope of state agencies, namely values, ideals and goals which can make an otherwise aimless life worthwhile.

Race relations

Any reader of the Bible will realise that resentment against racial minorities is not new. It seems, however, to have come into much sharper focus in many countries since the Second World War. Why this has happened is not fully understood, but it is probably due largely to better communications and facilities for travel which have tended to disrupt local communities, combined with vivid reporting of racial disorders by press and broadcasting, and the fact that racial minorities – or those who dislike them – can be important sources of votes in political elections.

The minorities resented appear to fall into two types. On the one hand are those which are, on average, more successful than the majority in an economic sense, such as Jews in Europe, Indians in East Africa and Chinese in South-East Asia: the feeling against these is the feeling against the successful of any race, namely a mixture of jealousy and of fear that their economic power will be used to oppress, by cornering markets or buying political influence. On the other hand are minorities which are resented because they have a lower average standard of living than the majority, such as African, Asian and Irish migrants in parts of Britain.

Although every reasonable man, and especially every Christian must, if he is true to his principles, deplore feelings against racial minorities, it has to be admitted that such feelings are not without some foundation. With regard to the first type of minority, sheer jealousy of the successful is to be condemned as tending to destroy achievement and to warp the objectivity with which one views the world. Yet some instances of commercial and political sharp practice by members of wealthy minority groups have been known to occur, although it is doubtful whether they have been more frequent among these minorities than in the population as a whole. As regards the second type of minority, insanitary living and overcrowded houses may be a threat to public health, and may depress the value of other houses in the same district so that their owners' savings are jeopardised. Again, by accepting low wages, members of a minority race may threaten rates of pay and increase competition for jobs, subsidised housing and welfare amenities. They also usually tend to have a high birthrate, so that there can be fear that, in a one-man-one-vote modern democracy, they will eventually take control at the polls.

We may, however, doubt whether such jealousies and fears would be associated with race as such, unless other factors were also at work. Among these factors, two which derive from human characteristics and limitations, seem especially important. The first is a well-known tendency to assume that any judgement made about one member of an identifiable class of objects or persons, can be applied to all members of the class. Thus, a man who has owned a car which has given trouble, may refuse ever to buy that make of car again, or a man who has been ill after eating a certain food will never eat it again. Such a tendency has obvious value as a means of minimising the risk of repeating undesirable experiences, but can go too far. The particular car may have been an unfortunate example of a very good make, and the food may have been stale or ill-prepared, but unless they are tried again, the man concerned will never know. Much the same tendency affects attitudes to other races or classes of people: one or two incidents associated with particular members are assumed to be typical of all. This is especially common when the members have some readily identifiable characteristic in common, such as skin colour.

The second factor making for racial disharmony is that there are, at the present time, substantial average differences between races in both customs and personal characteristics. Such differences have often been played down, or even denied, by those concerned to stress racial equality. The well-intentioned thinking of these people seems, however, to have been over-simple. We can rightly insist that members of all races are treated as equal before God and have equal opportunity to obtain justice from the law and to develop their talents, but such equality does not mean that all races are identical, any more than it implies that the members of any one race, or indeed of any one family, are identical. Looking at samples drawn as fairly as possible from different races, it is clear that several differences of mental and physical capacity and characteristics exist as average trends. There is, nevertheless, a wide scatter between individuals, so that many members of the race with lower average attainments, do better than many members of the race whose average attainments are higher, and vice versa. Any judgement based solely on average trends will, therefore, do less than justice to many individuals.

How far might present differences between races be abolished in the future? For example, would present racial trends disappear if the childhood experiences, economic circumstances and education of different races were fully equated? The answer to this question depends largely on whether racial differences are genetically determined, or result from environmental factors.

Almost certainly, both are involved to some extent. A large number of studies have shown that environmental factors are indeed important. However, genetic factors obviously lie behind differences of body build, shape of facial features and skin colour, and we might expect that there would, similarly, be genetically determined variations in the brain, which would affect temperament and styles of behaviour. Evidence that genetic factors can affect temperament and ability in domestic and laboratory animals is very clear: for example, aggressiveness and hunting abilities differ greatly between different breeds of dog; and strains of laboratory rat have been bred to be especially "bright" or "dull" at learning their way through mazes. Human genetic studies are inevitably less clear cut, but studies of identical twins reared apart have indicated that they have remarkable similarities of temperament, interests and even minor mannerisms (e.g. Kallmann, 1953, 1957).

The reduction or elimination of racial differences is obviously easier if they derive from environmental influences than if they are based on genetic factors; and it is therefore understandable that most of those who have been concerned to reduce racial tensions, have thought in terms of equating the social and economic conditions of different races. Insofar as genetic variations exist, however, such action is likely to be only partly successful. In any case, racial differences exist at the present time which, even if they are due to environmental factors, have been established in early childhood, and could not possibly be abolished in the present generation. We need, therefore, not to try to ignore racial differences, but instead to discover why they cause problems, and how these might be avoided.

Some racial antipathy may be due to irrational dislikes: for example, both negroes and white people are said to find the characteristic body odour of the other race more revolting than that of their own. The origin of such dislikes is obscure, and could well repay study, but they seem unlikely to be fundamental, since racial antipathies are usually less evident among young children than among adults – the antipathies seem to depend on developed experience.

This suggests that a more likely source of friction lies in different habits of everyday behaviour. For example, resentment seems frequently to arise when one race tends to make more noise than the other, or is noisy at times when the other wishes to be quiet. More subtly, when two races are living in close proximity, any differences between them of language, capacity or social customs, will make communication difficult, and will widen the variety of data with which any one person has to deal, thus increasing the complexity and uncertainty involved in everyday living. Lack of full communication and understanding will increase the likelihood of error in dealing with the opposite race, and this in turn may lead to fear and withdrawal. The whole situation tends towards the one which, at the beginning of the chapter, we suggested was typical of enmity. The problem will be particularly acute when there are actual conflicts of meaning: when, for instance, a style of dress implies one set of personal characteristics among one race, and another among the other; or when the same action is interpreted differently by different races, so that courses of action in the presence of the other race have to be chosen with extra care if they are not to be misunderstood.

If this view is correct, three implications follow which do, in fact, seem to hold broadly true. First, friction will arise most where substantial numbers of two or more races are living together in the same cities or neighbourhoods, so that they are having to take account of one another at all times (e.g. Kawwa, 1968): rare, isolated members of another race met for limited periods tend to excite curiosity and interest rather than enmity. Second, attempts to reduce the complications involved in living close to members of another race by means of partial segregation, are likely to be unsuccessful: they will cut the races off from one another, so that the uncertainty inherent in such contacts as remain will be increased. Third, the easiest relationships seem likely to exist when members of different races understand each other's reactions thoroughly.

The crucial question is, how to secure such mutual understanding. The task is not easy, but a few pointers and suggestions seem promising. Racial antagonisms tend to be reduced in the face of a common threat which, presumably, binds members of different races together in a joint aim (e.g. Burnstein & McRae, 1962). An American study has shown that white students show less antipathy to negroes of the same religious denomination as themselves, than they do to other negroes (Engel, 1968). Another American study has found that acquaintance with various types of negro, especially with those of relatively high occupational status, tends to engender favourable attitudes in white people, not only to the particular negroes they know, but to negroes in general (MacKenzie, 1948). This last point gives special emphasis to the need for equality of opportunity, given equal ability, in work, education and professional life.

On a broader scale, two main lines of action appear to be indicated, on psychological grounds, in order to foster the two-way communication needed for friendship, and to avoid the conditions of hostility. First, there is need for a great deal of instruction and education to break down language barriers, to train members of backward races in more civilised and hygienic methods of living, and to provide members of all races with accurate, sympathetic and unsentimental knowledge about other races' customs, problems, hopes and fears. Second, and even more fundamental, is the cultivation among members of all races, of what has sometimes worn thin in recent times, namely mutual forbearance, and respect for the privacy and values of the individual who differs from oneself.

THE NATURE OF CHRISTIAN LOVE

Almost everyone would agree that the most important of Christian virtues is love of God, shown and given concrete form in love of other people. Exactly what is meant by such love is, however, extremely difficult to say: everyone knows roughly what they mean by it, but it is one of those many terms in everyday use, such as intelligence, character or humour, which we never seem able to pin down precisely. It appears always to have been so, as is indicated by St. Paul's lengthy catalogue of its qualities in his first letter to the Corinthians (1 Corinthians 13). Can we, nineteen hundred years after, say any more? It seems fair to claim that we can, if only by way of exposition, and this we shall attempt to do as a way of summing up the general line of argument which has run through this chapter.

It is generally accepted that one of the main features of Christian love, is a looking away from oneself in a complete devotion to others – a giving of oneself without counting the cost. If, however, this were all, it could lead to the behaviour of a mother who overwhelms her child with affection, so that it becomes spoilt and selfish, and loses its initiative. This we cannot regard as Christian virtue at its highest, and must therefore reject as an example of Christian love.

The straightforward interpretation of the principle of: "Do unto others as you would they should do unto you" will not suffice either. It could lead to the kind of situation in which a keen academic invites a country-living girl friend to an important lecture on some abstruse corner of his subject. He would enjoy being asked to such a lecture by a colleague, but she will be bored. The case is a little better if we rephrase the principle to read: "Do unto others as they would you should do unto them." In this form, it pinpoints one important aspect of Christian love, namely putting oneself in the recipient's place. This, we may note in passing, is not an easy thing to do, and demands an effort of imagination which the more literal-minded and insensitive among us find it hard to achieve. The rephrasing is still, however, not sufficient. The beggars who come up in the street or visit welfare organisations, want to be given money, but it is doubtful whether giving it to them is an act of Christian love. Whatever story they tell, money given to them will almost certainly go for a drink, or on a horse. What they need is a type of psychiatric care which the health services of countries such as Britain do not yet provide, and money given to them would be better spent by voluntary bodies seeking to supply the kind of help needed. The beggars would not be grateful, but if anything is going to help them, it is this rather than cash in the hand.

Here, then, is a second important facet of Christian love: the need to look beyond the immediate desires of the present to the needs of the future, even if this means some denial and dissatisfaction at the moment. For example, the children of a famous psychologist were brought up according to what were, at the time, the latest ideas, to do what they liked and to express themselves freely so as to avoid the dangers of frustration and repression. When they grew up, they were highly critical of their father for not having made them work at the more tedious tasks at school, which would have opened a wider world to them in later life; and they made sure that their own children were disciplined enough to bring out their talents, and to enable them to do the things that would broaden their experience, deepen their insight, and qualify them for jobs suited to their abilities and interests.

There is, nevertheless, a grave danger in trying to do better for others than they themselves know. Many religious persecutions have been conducted with the sincere desire to save men's souls, despite themselves. Some judgement of what is best for others is inevitable if one is to love them fully, but it needs to be made humbly, without any trace of arrogance, and after the most searching thought possible. We arrive, therefore, at the conclusion that Christian love involves not only, nor indeed mainly, feeling and emotions, but is an intellectual exercise as severe as any we ever encounter.

What is more, good intentions and even right conclusions, are not enough. We have not only to love, but to make our love effective. This means that we have to treat people in the way we outlined as characteristic of friendship, building up a two-way communication with them, so that they are able and willing to accept what is offered, and to benefit from it. For this, we not only need an insight into the other person's needs, values, capacities and interests, but must also pay attention to matters of elementary tact and technique, taking care to avoid actions or ways of putting statements which might hurt the other's self-esteem, and trying to make appropriate choices of occasions and moments on which to speak and act. Much of this can be achieved by attention to some of the ordinary rules of courtesy and etiquette. The more robust of these represent a codification over the years of techniques found effective as ways to avoid trampling on other people's personalities.

More important still, we need a genuine sympathy, and a patent honesty and reliability of character, such that other people will feel that their confidences will never be betrayed, and our advice will never have ulterior motives – the qualities shown, for instance, by an employer who will encourage an employee to take a better job even if he is hard to replace, or by parents who do not dissuade their grown-up children from leaving home, even if it means loneliness and a major reshaping of their own lives. Perhaps most of all, we need the breadth of vision to see each day-to-day event, and every personal relationship, not as isolated and for the moment, but in the wider framework of space and time, larger than ourselves and longer than our own lives, that we have in an earlier chapter defined as God.

Chapter VII

Worthwhileness of Life

IN THIS chapter we shall use the concepts of coding, feedback and loading that we have outlined in previous chapters, to look at a range of problems generally recognised as of pressing importance in the world today. They can be broadly divided into three classes according to whether they derive from increase of population, expansion of knowledge or advances in large-scale organisation. We shall deal with each class in turn.

INCREASE OF POPULATION

It is well known that advances in medicine which are enabling more people to survive into old age, and earlier marriage, have led to a rapid rise in the world's population. This promises, at existing rates of fertility, to accelerate in the next few years. Advances in agriculture have removed any immediate likelihood that these increased numbers will starve for lack of food, although other problems such as shortage of water are becoming pressing. There is an immediate problem, however, in the greater crowding of people in habitable areas, and the effects of this on the quality of life.

The relationships between crowding and quality of life are complex, and seem to depend both on economic factors and on the reactions of individuals to crowding as such. From the economic point of view, a very sparse population leads to a low level of material culture, because the tasks of establishing a viable control of nature over a large area by a few people, means that there is little chance of specialisation, or time for activities which are not of obvious urgency. As population increases, these limitations ease, and the quality of life improves. Above a certain optimum density, however, quality of life begins to fall again in a number of respects. In part, this is due to increased pollution of the natural environment – a tendency which is difficult to control, because measures to combat it mean taking trouble and spending money with little or no immediate return. The major economic difficulty of crowding, however, seems to be the competition it generates for scarce resources – from housing at a reasonable price, to parking for one's car, a bench in the park or a seat in a bus. It has to be remembered, however, that along with these difficulties go a number of continued improvements. For example, it is only in large cities that theatres, opera houses and the other amenities of a rich and varied cultural life, can be sustained on a substantial scale. The economic effects of high concentration are thus mixed, and no one level will be optimum in all respects.

More fundamental from a psychological point of view, are the effects of social contacts on individual behaviour. We have already noted that these tend to be arousing and activating. Overall, their effects run parallel to those of economic factors with rise in the density of population. As we move from a sparse population to a moderate concentration, the increased social stimulation tends to make individuals more alert, and to improve their performance generally. High concentrations seem, however, to have some less satisfactory results. Experimental studies have shown that animals kept under crowded conditions tend to develop abnormally large adrenal glands, to fight, and to show tension, irritation and other signs of stress. Much the same tendencies can be detected, as average trends, among human beings living in large cities, when compared with those living in country districts. Some of these stress symptoms are doubtless due to the struggle to obtain a share of resources in short supply, but most of them seem to derive directly from the activation and arousal which arise from contact with others. Once again, some of the effects of the resulting tension are desirable and some not. For less sensitive people, especially when engaged on simple tasks, relatively high levels of stress are necessary to bring out their abilities to the full. The performance of those who are more highly strung, however, tends to be impaired, especially at more complex tasks, and they may suffer ill health from psychosomatic disease.

Perhaps more important than the immediate stress effects of crowding, are the results of what seem to be efforts to mitigate them. Individuals seem to try spontaneously to adjust their arousal to an optimum level. Thus, those whose normal level is low, tend to seek social contacts, and to enjoy loud noises, bright colours and stimulating situations. Those whose normal level is high, tend to seek peace, quiet and isolation (Hebb, 1955, see also Welford, 1968, chapter 10). The overstimulation of crowded conditions thus produces unwitting attempts by many people to minimise social contacts. As a result, people in large cities tend to make relatively few deep friendships, and those who do not find social acquaintance easy may be isolated. Such isolation in the midst of crowding has the further effect of making it easy for an individual to melt into the crowd, so that crime becomes difficult to detect, and is thus safer and more likely to be rewarding.

These same factors tend also, on a broader scale, to encourage war. It is fair to argue that competition for scarce resources has been by far the commonest cause of war, although it has seldom if ever been a sufficient cause. Of the necessary additional causes, one of the most frequent seems to have been severe overcrowding in the country which starts the war. Like other results of crowding, the effects of war are mixed. The most obvious is the indiscriminate destruction and degradation, which make war repugnant to any reasonable person. At the same time, it has to be admitted that the courage, dedication and sense of purpose war has given to many individual lives, means that its results have not been as wholly negative as is commonly supposed: history is full of wars in which people have been willing to put freedom and integrity above life itself, and have thereby not only preserved these qualities for their heirs, but developed their own potential worth.

How can the unsatisfactory effects of overcrowding and the consequent danger of war be avoided? Four main possibilities have commonly been suggested. The first of these is that there should be a radical and world-wide change in human nature and values. This, however desirable it might be, must be dismissed as unrealistic, at least for the foreseeable future. Human beings are probably not as cruel as they were a century ago, but clearly they have a long way still to go before violence, crime, greed and short-sighted policy-making are eliminated. A more modest suggestion is that attempts should be made to secure a more even distribution of the world's wealth. This might reduce the risk of war to some extent, but would by no means eliminate it: for example, aggressive nations might well still fight to obtain more than their allotted share. In any case, it would do nothing to solve the individual problems of crowding. A third policy is that of decentralising population, by migration from over-populated countries and moving people away from large cities into smaller towns. This policy has a considerable appeal, but it would be quite inadequate to solve the world's present problems, and would entail substantial difficulties and losses to be set against any advantages that might be gained. For example, to flood Australia with Asian migrants, would destroy the present Australian way of life, without alleviating the population problems of the countries of Asia to any appreciable extent. On a smaller scale, the dispersion of population from large cities to a host of small towns, would make the provision of cultural and other amenities almost impossibly expensive in both resources and manpower.

In the long run, the only way of relieving over-crowding, and thus minimising the risk of stress diseases and war, is by limiting the production of children. The task is, admittedly, not easy. On the social scale, political power tends gradually to pass to that section of the population which has the highest birth rate. Many sectional interests are, therefore, unwilling to do anything that would tend to reduce their numbers. For example, several political parties in Europe would, in time, be weakened if sanctions against birth control were abandoned by certain church denominations.

Before effective methods of birth control were available, control of population had to include abstinence from sexual intercourse, and we may perhaps view the aversion from sex in late nineteenth century Europe, as an unconscious recognition that population there was beginning to exceed the resources then available. Now that birth control methods are effective, this attitude is no longer necessary. The main problem of population control now seems to lie in the deep-seated desire, mentioned in the previous chapter, of men and women, especially the latter, to produce and possess children. This seemingly instinctive, "fleshly" urge is shared by lower animals, and control of it is probably the most important task confronting the world today.

How this can be done we do not yet know fully, but it appears that there is a broad tendency for birth rates to fall, especially in under-developed countries, when there is a rise in the standard of living: presumably people are content with fewer children when there are other things to do and work for. Two further suggestions which follow from points we have already made, seem also to be germane. First, a childless life is not to be condemned as "selfish" or "unnatural". Childlessness was recognised in the New Testament as an opportunity for service to the community that would not otherwise be possible, and it still is today. For example, a man with children cannot well take a job which prevents him from having a settled home. Again, celibate orders in the Church have, on the whole, a good record of service to others. The same would probably prove to be true of childless marriages.

Second, and more generally important, is the need to insist that children should be produced only when there is reasonable assurance of a sound, stable upbringing. This means that parents who have a child, must accept not only the satisfactions of parenthood, but also the often heavy responsibilities. They must, for example, face the fact that they will have less money to spend on themselves, will be less free to come and go as they like, will have to take holidays in a manner suitable for the children rather than themselves, and will suffer many worries and disappointments. The present need is for quality rather than quantity of children and, since man cannot well impose upon his own kind the selective breeding he practices with domestic animals, the main responsibility for quality must rest with parents.

EXPANSION OF KNOWLEDGE

One of the most striking and important changes that have occurred in developed countries since about 1960 has been the rapid increase in the amount of research published. To take only one example, 8,532 articles were listed in Psychological Abstracts for 1960. In 1952 there had been 7,297, so that the increase over the eight years had been about 17 per cent. Eight years later, however, in 1968, there were 19,586 items listed – an increase of 130 per cent. Similar accelerations have occurred in other fields of science. The new knowledge they represent is to be welcomed, as opening the way to greater technological control over nature, the mitigation of many hardships of life and, most of all, comprehension of truth. It does, however, at the same time, bring a number of problems which must be solved before its full benefits can be reaped.

The most obvious of these problems is that man has acquired powers which are potentially dangerous, as well as beneficial. The best recognised examples are nuclear energy which can be used for atomic bombs, as well as holding out hope for power to make deserts fertile by desalinating sea water; and chemical pesticides, which have controlled many diseases, but can also be a hazard to health. Closer to everyday experience, powerful cars have given a flexibility to travel never before known, but have taken a serious toll of life and caused many disastrous brain injuries in the hands of thoughtless drivers.

A different kind of problem arises from the fact that the amount of knowledge relevant to any academic discipline or professional qualification is now so large that both student and teacher are under great strain. They are much more heavily loaded than they were even as short a time ago as the 1950s. As a result, there has to be greater specialisation, which tends to cut down communication, and to isolate those engaged in academic or professional studies into tightly-knit groups. At the same time, the effort to preserve a reasonable breadth of grasp means that students and teachers have so much reading to do that they have little time for the discussion and leisurely, informal contacts traditional in academic life. Students have, in consequence, felt neglected, and have increasingly suffered from stress symptoms and breakdowns.

Many teachers in senior positions have failed to keep up with developments, and the same has often been true of those occupying senior positions in industry, politics and various forms of administration. The inevitable pressures of work on those who carry responsibility make it tempting to ignore new facts and ideas, so as to save the time and trouble involved in adapting their thinking and policies. This does not matter much when the flow of new knowledge is small, but is very serious with the present rate of increase. It means that younger men in junior positions often have a better grip of their work than their seniors. This in turn leads to breakdown of the normal respect for age, so that the benefits of long experience, and the subtleties of understanding that it brings, may be swept aside in an overriding desire to keep up to date, by getting rid of dead wood at the top.

The substitution of fact for opinion has increased the demand that rational justification should be given for actions and policies. This is often difficult to do in a convincing manner, not because of any obscurantism or muddle-headedness, but because the reasons for subtle, complex, intuitive judgements are not fully conscious. Correct action in complex situations, often involves the weighing of a mass of facts, possibilities, risks and potential advantages, which the "neural computers" of our brains can handle accurately, but are unable to spell out in detail on demand. If this is not recognised, increase of knowledge can result in an undermining of authority, and the insistence that the need for every demand or prohibition should be proved to the satisfaction of the individuals to whom it applies, before they consider it to be binding. Such a requirement not only wastes the powers of some of the community's most valuable intellects, but is unrealistic, in the sense that proof before action is still far from possible except on a very limited scale: the great majority of life has still to be governed by hypothesis, intuition and the authority of experience, rather than by proven fact. Failure to recognise this is probably the reason why many young people arrogantly reject their parents' standards and over-value their own powers (Shapiro, 1957, Shippee-Blum, 1959).

It is easy to become so obsessed with these various dangers, that one loses sight of the benefits of knowledge, and seeks to reject it or to feel, hopelessly, that it is impossible to control it and use it aright. An example is the failure of courage seen in many young people, because of the potential danger of war. Both rejection and hopelessness imply a lack of Christian faith as we have defined it in Chapter IV (p. 89). The success and strength of Christianity, as opposed to other religious or non-religious creeds, can in large part be traced to its insistence that Christians go out actively to embrace the world with all its problems, learning to use its facilities while combating its dangers. In relation to the expansion of modern knowledge, this aim implies four needs:

First, we have to recognise that, because a thing *can* be done, it is not necessary that it *should* be done. In the days when man's powers were less, it was a sound and progressive attitude to assume that everything possible should be tried. Now instead, we need to consider priorities and long-term consequences, to an extent that has never been required of any previous generation. Both individuals and groups must exercise an unprecedented degree of self-restraint. It is also more important than ever before to restrain, by force if necessary, those aggressive, perverse or mischievous people who wish to misuse their powers.

Second, there is a need to codify present knowledge. This involves concentrating on the broad principles running through many different studies, leaving finer details to be examined only when necessary for special purposes. Even more, it means that teachers have a duty continually to prune out of their courses everything that is unnecessary. This can sometimes require the abandonment of material on which the teacher has expended a great deal of thought, and on which he may feel that much of his academic expertise rests. If so, he is in the same position as the industrial tradesman, who finds that a change of manufacturing process has made his skill redundant. Both teacher and tradesman can find this situation acutely distressing, but it is one that has to be faced.

Third, and following from this last point, there is need to accept the fact that what is learnt at school, university or college, or in an apprenticeship, is only a beginning: anyone who is to remain expert in any field has to relearn it continually during his lifetime. The magnitude of the task is greater than many people realise: for instance, almost all the subject-matter taught in undergraduate courses of psychology and several other sciences, has changed during the twenty-five years or so since those in senior positions were themselves students. Again, from the industrial point of view, the use of computers and virtually the whole of the aircraft, electronics, plastics and synthetic fibre industries, have grown up since present-day senior management started work as young men. For some, the changes come gradually, and for them the need is to keep their routine work and the administrative responsibilities that tend to accumulate in middle-age, to a level such that time can still be set aside for reading, discussion and thought. Further, they must be willing to have their preconceived ideas disturbed from time to time by new developments, and to live with the resulting uncertainties until they have been able to reorder their thinking. For others, the need to relearn is more sudden and complete, due to a change of job or a breakthrough in ideas or techniques. It is often assumed that such relearning becomes impossible beyond young adulthood, but this is not true. A number of industrial studies have shown that people can and do learn well in middle-age, provided suitable training methods are used (E. Belbin, 1964, R. M. Belbin, 1965, 1969). The essential requirement seems to be to ensure that older trainees discover information or methods of work for themselves, while making sure that mistakes are either prevented, or quickly corrected so that they do not become ingrained.

Fourth, and above all, is the need for humility and a sense of responsibility, in recognising both the power and the limitations of present knowledge. We need to acknowledge that, while researches in many fields have yielded truth to an extent never known before, they have also yielded some errors, and even when correct, have often been grossly over-interpreted. There is therefore a need for both courage to accept change, and for caution in deciding when it is justified. While failure of the first leads to sterility, lack of the second can impair the stability which is necessary if men are to have confidence, and to live and work effectively.

The potentialities and problems of increased knowledge in recent years affect the Church in two ways. First, psychology and the social sciences have provided a wide range of ideas and techniques, which could well be applied to the organisation of church work and the conduct of its teaching. Second, and of more obvious impact, is the need to take much greater care than is usual at present, to present Christian ideas in such a way that they can be comprehended and accepted by those of an enquiring, critical, scientifically oriented mind. For this, the prime need seems to be to spell out *reasons* for precepts and doctrines. It is not enough, for example, to say that an action is "immoral": rather it is necessary to state, with evidence, the probable consequences of the action concerned. Again, it is not enough to speak of an action as "in accordance with the will of God": there must be a clear definition of what is meant by "the will of God", coupled with a precise indication of how the action concerned exemplifies it. Perhaps hardest for many to accept, is that we can no longer invoke the Bible in its present form as an absolute authority. At the very least, we need to use all the means of scholarship at our disposal, to discover what the original authors were trying to say, and to consider their statements in the context of their own time. More important, we need to recognise that the Bible has authority insofar as its key ideas are found to be valid for the daily lives of ordinary men and women. Our interpretation must begin with the attempt to assess the nature and extent of this validity.

Medical advances

One of the areas in which the advance of knowledge has been most spectacular, has been in medicine and medical care. Antibiotics and other drugs, immunisation and better public health have virtually ended the toll that was taken before the Second World War by diseases such as tuberculosis, sepsis, diptheria and poliomyelitis. As a result, many more people are living on to grow old, instead of dying in early life or middle-age. This development has had obvious benefits in reducing the waste of valuable lives, which were previously cut off before they had realised their full potential, but it has brought with it two urgent problems.

First, more and more people are living a substantial portion of their lives after their main work has been done — for men a period of retirement, for women a time after their children have grown up and left home. Both frequently report that they "feel useless" and need, but have difficulty in acquiring, new interests and activities. What appears to have happened is that their principal sources of two-way traffic with the environment

—work-mates for a man and children for a woman—are no longer available, so that motivation fails. These feelings do not depend, to any appreciable extent, on the economic or material circumstances of the people concerned, but on their attitudes to life and to other people. The lonely and disgruntled are mainly those who fail to take opportunities for a full life, and to avail themselves of social contacts that are offered to them: instead they are jealous, demanding, self-centred or complaining (Reichard *et al.* 1962). They are, in short, those who adopt attitudes which inhibit the two-way traffic of friendship with neighbours and acquaintances, which could be a substitute for the previous feedback from work-mates or family.

The search for methods of rescuing people from this state, or preventing them from falling into it, would seem to be an important field for Christian work. The task is not easy, however, and will not be achieved by the provision of old people's clubs, or the teaching of hobbies before retirement. The outgoing interests implied by membership of clubs and by hobbies are the result, rather than the cause, of realistic and satisfying attitudes in old age. These in turn seem to depend on facets of personality developed much earlier in life: those who enjoy their old age and find retirement rewarding, are those who have had a realistic and contented attitude to life, and have maintained easy two-way traffic with others before retirement. Those, on the other hand, who are disagreeable or disgruntled have always been so, although these failings have often been hidden in earlier years by the customs, formalities and enforced social contacts of work and family. The basic problem of retirement is thus one of mastery of one's own emotions and desires, so as to ensure continued contact with others, and is a task to be begun at birth, and continued throughout life.

The second problem raised by increased length of life is more fundamental. Consider the true case of an elderly woman who, after leading an independent life which had been useful and had given pleasure to many, became senile. First she grew disagreeable, and bottles of port had to be hidden from her; then she became vague about who people were; soon she started to wander, to tear off her clothes and to become incontinent, and in this state she lingered for some two years before she died. By then she had ceased to be the person any of her relatives or friends had known. It was obvious from an early stage that her condition was irreversible and terminal. One may fairly ask just when it really was that she, as an individual person, died? Was it indeed two days before her funeral, or had she been, in a sense, dead long before? If so, what ought to have been done? Should she have been kept alive in an essentially vegetative state by hospital care, as she had been, or should she have been allowed to depart earlier? These are questions that no previous generation has had to face to anything like the same extent as ours. They are part of a larger question, which includes not only the senile, but also those whose brains are severely damaged in accidents and have no hope of anything approaching full recovery, and infants who are born with gross brain deficiencies or damage, which will preclude them from ever leading a full and independent life. Should any of these have their existence prolonged, when they can never be restored to normality?

The cost of the intensive care such patients need is high, but in the end, it is manpower rather than money that is the limitation. Nurses and doctors are in short supply, and waiting lists for hospital beds are long. These patients are, in fact, competing with others who, with a fraction of the same care, could be restored to full health. Should these latter have to wait for treatment, possibly getting worse for lack of it? Should they waste months, or sometimes years, of life in order to prolong the mere existence of those who can never again be their full selves?

The medical shortage could, perhaps, be overcome if manpower and resources were transferred from other activities, such as education, welfare, office work and manufacturing industry, but it is doubtful whether the people concerned would be suitable for medical work or would do it willingly, even if there was general agreement that priorities between medical and other needs should be adjusted in this way.

The stark question of priorities arises again if, as is often suggested, care is not given by nurses in hospital, but by relatives at home. Many patients need virtually the full-time attention of one person. Is it right to take the whole of one person's life over a period of years, to maintain the bare survival of another who can have no future except a gradual decline to death? If that relative has other family responsibilities which have to be neglected to look after the patient, the answer seems clear, but even if she (the person is usually a woman) has not, is her life well spent looking after, say, a senile, incontinent mother?

Again, caring for a mentally defective child may take virtually the whole time of its mother, and we may well ask how much of someone else's life is worth expending on an existence that can never attain any reasonable quality? Even if a mother looking after such a child at home manages also to bring up other, normal children, the presence of an abnormal child may warp their outlook, since they may be unable to entertain friends, and are likely to get less than their share of maternal care – a neglect which may in turn lead to lack of achievement and even to delinquency and other social difficulties. At the very least, it seems kinder to the family as a whole, and a more efficient deployment of people's lives, if a defective child is placed in a special institution. Would it not be better still if it had not survived?

Some doctors quietly administer an over-dose of drug to some terminal patients, or deliberately fail to revive an accident victim or to allow a gravely impaired infant to breathe—acts of mercy for which all concerned should be grateful. Many people, however, would regard such actions as murder, or at least as an over-stepping of medical responsibility. Whether they are so or not, depends largely on the definition of death.

Normally, death is regarded as having occurred when there is an irreversible cessation of bodily function, such that disintegration of the body will follow. Recently, especially in France, it has been argued that the individual as a whole is dead when his brain is dead—that is when the seat of his personality and of the co-ordination of his thought and action which make him a human being, has irreversibly ceased to function. Both these definitions are essentially in functional terms, so that we arrive at a concept of life as a state of functional integrity. We may, therefore, ask whether death should perhaps be regarded as having occurred following other functional impairments, short of total death of the brain. If, however, we look at death in this way, two difficulties at once arise. First, it can be rightly argued that in making judgements about whether or not to let people survive, we are on a slippery slope. Where do we draw the line? How certainly can we predict non-recovery? Advances in medical understanding make such predictions much better than they were even a few years ago, but it is doubtful if they are yet sufficiently accurate to be used in making judgements of such finality. Clinicians could here reasonably look to psychologists for objective tests to help them. Tests presently available are sketchy, but it is already routine to use behavioural measurements or assessments as an aid to the diagnosis of brain damage, and some preliminary studies of old people have shown how survival is associated with level of intellectual functioning (Birren, 1965). If the challenge was issued, the tests available would no doubt improve.

The second difficulty arising from a definition of death in terms of mental integrity, lies in guilt feelings which might arise from not doing everything possible to preserve the last vestiges of life. This was not a great problem when little effective could be done, but now seems often to be felt if the utmost resources are not employed regardless of cost. Guilt is understandable, if sometimes mistaken, among hospital staff when they do not make full use of their professional expertise. It can also be understood among relatives if they take decisions which seem to run counter to natural affections, and this may be exacerbated by criticisms from friends and neighbours who are often, alas, all too ready to score a point. How far guilt feelings could be prevented or overcome is difficult to say, but we may note as possible leads that these seem commonly to arise most in people who least deserve them, and that hard thinking about emotionally toned questions can often bring an objectivity which is neither callous nor insensitive.

Many religious people, both Christians and others, would be acutely unhappy at the line of argument developed here. Three main types of objection are likely to be advanced: First, there is value in suffering, and it is therefore right that people should face distress and calamity. Second, man should not tamper with the works of God. Third, man is made in the image of God and has, therefore, an inherent dignity and potentiality for salvation, which must at all costs be preserved: since death destroys these, life must be prolonged as far as possible. By the same tokens, human beings, however much they are born with original sin, are inherently good in their potential and, therefore, the more of them the better.

The first two of these objections seem, on examination, to be misconceived. Certainly some suffering is needed to bring out the best in any individual. For example, it is stunting to a child's mental and emotional development to protect it from all struggle, worry, pain and disappointment. It would be wrong, however, to conclude from this that all suffering brings gain. During the last twenty years we have come to realise that stresses and anxieties can be beneficial in small doses, either intense for a short time or milder for a longer period, but can be devastating to both mental and physical integrity if intense and unremitting, especially if they do not point to a way of future escape. The sufferings engendered by the problems of life and death that we have been discussing are of this latter kind, and while they may occasionally yield rare moral insight, their effects are all too likely to be degrading rather than edifying.

The second objection is again too sweeping. It is true that some of man's tampering with nature has not been entirely fortunate in its results, but if all attempts to manipulate nature were disallowed, we should have to rule out not only agriculture, stock-breeding and civil engineering, but also education and medicine — activities which the Church has traditionally fostered. In short, many tamperings with nature are good rather than bad, in both their intentions and their effects, and represent working with, rather than against God.

The third objection is the most important, but appears to clarify and sharpen, rather than destroy, the case for thinking again about the nature of life and death. It means that, when making decisions about individuals, we must be careful in our assessment of whether or not a patient will recover, whether or not an impairment at birth can be adequately overcome. However, it does nothing to solve the problem of priorities: for example, continuation of mere existence may give a patient a remote chance of significant recovery which will prolong his time of potential spiritual development, yet the medical service and education for normal people with which his case might be competing for resources, may preserve or realise the potentialities of people with much more future opportunity before them.

Perhaps the nub of the argument lies in what is meant by "the image of God" and the human dignity that derives from it. For this to mean the integrity of the body, is patently absurd: if it did, the image of God would take some strangely distorted forms, many of the greatest saints would not qualify, and surgery would be a sin. It must mean something less tangible than this, and the nearest modern translation of the phrase seems to come very close to what we think of as mental and emotional integrity. If so, when these are lost or lacking, should we not say that the surviving body no longer bears the image of God, and is in a religious sense, indeed dead? In other words, the religious stand is valid, but the definitions of life and death adopted by religious people are called into question.

ADVANCES IN ORGANISATION

Perhaps the most far-reaching, and also the most immediately important, changes in civilised life over the last few decades have been the co-ordination of effort by larger and larger groups of people, and the harnessing of vast economic resources. These have, in turn, led to increasingly effective use of the world's expanding knowledge, and produced an affluence almost undreamt of before the Second World War. All this must be hailed as a major advance. It has removed or mitigated many hardships, widened potentialities for self-realisation, and increased the material standard of life for the great majority of people – the modest comfort of a generation ago is regarded as poverty today. Yet, like many other advances, it has revealed difficulties which had hitherto been hidden or not fully recognised, and which make it clear that further progress is needed.

They are of two main kinds: the effects of affluence on motivation, and the constraints that organisation imposes on individuals.

Effects of affluence

In developed countries, the affluence of the last few years has meant that the necessities of life are now obtained with little effort. Jobs have been relatively easy to find, pay has been high, and in countries such as Britain, the welfare state has been ready to support anyone whose capacity for work fails. Nobody who saw the depression of the 1930s can regret this. Yet for many individuals, this security has led to reluctance to carry responsibility or to undertake difficult or tedious tasks, and unwillingness to undergo the training needed to acquire the skills on which the continuation of affluence depends. The feedback loop between the world and the individual has, in effect, been broken because reward has come to bear relatively little relation to effort. Life has therefore become insipid and boring. As a result, some people become indolent, doing the minimum required to obtain the substantial basic living the affluent society provides. Others, reacting against the "flatness" of life, seek stimulation in ways which demand relatively little effort, such as by gambling or driving cars fast, or by exploiting the bodily excitements of sex, drug-taking and violence. The seeking tends to be for this immediate bodily stimulation rather than anything less direct (Hocking and Robertson, 1969). It is associated with signs of hostility, as we should expect if it was due to the breaking of the feedback loop (Blackburn, 1969). It has also been found to be greater, on the one hand, in people of active but relatively insensitive personality (Zuckerman *et al.* 1964, Farley & Farley, 1967), and on the other, amongst those of higher intelligence and education (Kish & Busse, 1968): all characteristics which are associated with intolerance of monotony and boredom.

A further, indirect result of affluence, and of the seeking for stimulation that it brings, is an inversion of some important traditional values. For example, the public desire for excitement leads newspapers to offer large sums of money for the stories of spectacular crimes and scandals, or for the serial rights of books calculated to shock. It becomes a reasonable question to ask whether a prison sentence might not be worthwhile, if the story which led up to it could earn an investment which would yield a comfortable living for life, or a spectacular fling for a year or two. It becomes tempting to write a book which makes a deliberate, even if grossly unfair, attack on established and cherished ideas, when the serial rights alone will bring, perhaps, twenty times the earnings of a book of sober scholarship. Again, the earnings of, say, a schoolteacher who works hard and faithfully to bring out the potentialities of her pupils, come to compare even less favourably than they have done in the past, with those of the prostitute who topples a cabinet minister.

Effects of constraint

In Russia, and seemingly in other communist countries, there is a great deal of propaganda emphasising the need for individuals to conform, and the state has built up machinery to ensure that this occurs, and to punish deviant behaviour, to an extent that would be intolerable in the Western world (van der Post, 1964). Yet even in free countries, constraints on the individual are substantial, and seem to be growing. They are of many kinds. A simple and obvious example is that of the production-line factory worker, whose pace and method of work are rigidly dictated by the machinery he uses, who has little or no knowledge of preceding or succeeding stages in the production process, and who is thus aptly described as a "cog in the machine". Less obvious but more important, is the highly efficient sorting of children in terms of ability, which is made at various stages in their education. The ablest are selected out from the rest, and impelled at high pressure up through secondary school and university; while the less able are left with restricted prospects and, seemingly, little hope of advancement. This is especially the case since the expansion of knowledge has led to formal qualifications being demanded for an ever wider range of jobs. Courses leading to these qualifications often have prerequisites extending well back into school days, so that if the necessary examinations have not been passed at school, the doors ahead are very difficult to open. Whether the individual is especially able and pushed forward, or is less so and held back, he feels himself to be "caught up in the system".

Even the increases of freedom which result from affluence may be coupled with additional constraints. For example, possession of a car implies not only the freedom to travel more easily at times of one's own choosing, but also the responsibility for licensing it, for keeping it in repair, and for driving in a manner which conforms, at least substantially, to the rule of the road and fits in with the behaviour of other road users. Many people also feel that, because they own a car, it must be used, so that every weekend they drive to a beach or other pleasure resort, and no longer do any of the other things, such as walking or working in the garden, that they were free to do before they bought their cars. Again, hire-purchase agreements, while they enable people to enjoy goods before they can pay for them, impose a continuing burden of keeping up payments, which may, in turn, mean working long hours of overtime and anxiety if the opportunity to do so is not available.

The most serious constraints upon individuals probably arise when groups take collective action, or engage in collective negotiation. These can result in substantial personal satisfaction for the individuals who act as leaders or organisers, and there may be some sense of achievement for the rank and file when the results are greater than any one person could have achieved by his own unaided efforts. Most collective action, however, implies a compromise between the different desires or needs of many individuals, so that satisfaction for any one individual is never likely to be complete. Further, it is obviously impossible for a large group to act with every member present, so that decisions have to be taken through delegates. It is all too easy for these to be unrepresentative of the main body of members – they will often be the loudest mouthed or the most militant. They may also, whether consciously or unwittingly, be swayed by party loyalties against their better judgement, or use their positions for their own ends. In any case, a system of delegates or representatives, inevitably reduces the feedback between the individual and the organisation of which he is a member. Usually, for instance, his part is limited to casting a vote, after which he is powerless until the next election. Before this takes place, many irrevocable decisions may have been made, over which he has no direct control. Even if delegates report back to those who elected them, it is usually too late, or the delegate is too remote, for the individual to secure any change of decision.

Experimental studies of both animals and human beings suggest that severely constraining situations may lead to one of two different results, according to circumstances. First, the obstacles they place in the way of achievement, and the feeling they bring of acting under compulsion, may reduce motivation: keenness and persistence tend to be higher for tasks undertaken voluntarily, than for those done at someone else's command (Battle, 1965, Brock & Becker, 1967). In such circumstances an individual will often try to withdraw from the situation altogether. In a mild form, this attempt may lead to the use of a weekend cottage or the taking of holidays in remote places to "get away from it all". Less benign forms may lead to ignoring of the demands of society, which in turn produces inconsiderate behaviour towards others, and failure to respect the law. In extreme cases, there may be mental breakdown, or attempts to escape into the unreal worlds of alcohol or drugs (Gilbert & Lombardi, 1967), or to contract out of life, by becoming a tramp or a hippie.

Second, if withdrawal is impossible, the individual is likely to become irritable and tense, and to break out or rebel with more or less violence. Mild rebellion may take the form of sneering remarks at "the rat race" or "the system", and general expressions of disrespect for custom, tradition and "the establishment". A little stronger are activities such as smoking by young children (Stewart & Livson, 1966), or deliberate adoption by adolescents of unorthodox behaviour. The wearing of dirty clothes or long hair are easy ways of achieving some sort of individuality, and of annoying parents, teachers, employers and others who are regarded as sources of constraint. Such signs of rebellion shade into more serious attempts to be a nuisance. Among students, these include sit-ins and protest marches directed against constraining agencies, such as university administrations or the machinery of conscription to the armed services. In industry, they include wildcat strikes which, especially on production lines and in transport, can achieve spectacular stoppages with relatively little effort. Such deliberate and planned protests can, in more serious cases, give way to violent attempts to vent feelings on anything or anybody conveniently within reach and, in the extreme, to organised anarchy with a view to "smashing present society".

The degree of violence with which rebellion occurs seems

likely to depend on the degree of parental discipline in childhood. We have already noted in Chapter VI (p. 119) that permissiveness by parents tends to produce aggressiveness in children, presumably because children brought up permissively, have had less training in self-restraint. It seems fair to suggest also that there is a more subtle effect in the *changes* of demand made during adolescence upon children who are brought up in different ways. A child brought up strictly is able to look forward to a progressively greater freedom and relaxation of constraint, as he grows up through his teens to adulthood. Lack of discipline in early childhood means, however, that the teens and adult years will bring increasing constraints as educational demands and the responsibilities of work, and eventually marriage and parenthood, have to be met. Gradual breaking away from parental control is a natural and necessary part of the process of growing up, and seems to be sought on a relative basis. Thus for a very strictly disciplined child, quite modest relaxations will appear to confer substantial freedom, while a child who has had a permissive upbringing needs to resort to more violent acts of rebellion in order to assert its independence.

Regaining freedom

Avoidance or reduction of the various difficulties that arise from affluence or constraint, seems to depend on restoring an effective two-way traffic between the individual and his world, enabling him to influence the events around him, and ensuring that care and effort bring a due reward. Six courses of action seem to be required.

First, every individual should have the opportunity to develop and use his potentialities as fully as possible, and should be rewarded insofar as he employs them usefully, whether his gifts lie in academic scholarship, technical skill, social competence or any other form of worthwhile expertise. This, in turn, implies the need to match interest and aptitude to occupation, so that each individual's work presents a challenge to which he is capable of rising. There is a substantial contribution to be made here by psychologists practising vocational guidance and selection.

Second, the realisation of potential requires a measure of self-control. This is most easily built up in childhood, and therefore has implications for the training methods used by parents and teachers. Broadly speaking, they need to provide firm and reasoned guidance, together with feedback to the child about whether or not its performance has been adequate, and must take steps to ensure that the child pays attention to this feedback. It is also desirable that the child's efforts should not bring too great a result for effort expended. The total burden upon a child or adolescent should probably be such that life is not easier for it than for an adult, taking into consideration that children and adolescents do not have the full powers of intellect and personality possessed by adults, and may suffer from many worries and difficulties, due to ignorance and limited perspectives, that adults are spared.

Third, every organised system should be carefully designed, so that the constraints it places upon individuals are the minimum necessary, and can be seen to be justified. The contributions of industrial psychologists, work-study engineers, ergonomists and operational research workers are relevant here, not only in industry, but in the design of administrative procedures in offices and in government, and of flow-systems in hospitals, transport and on the road. The same experts can make important improvements in the design of many consumer products, so that they are more comfortable and convenient to use.

Fourth, where conformity is necessary, studies of motivation suggest that non-conformity should, if possible, not be punished, but should never be rewarded. For example, irresponsible protests seem to become more vigorous when punished, but tend to collapse quickly if no notice is taken of them, and if they are ignored by press, radio and television.

Fifth, individuals should have maximum freedom during leisure time, compatible with similar freedom for others. This implies that there should be not only opportunity for a range of recreations and hobbies, but also freedom from interference by others in the form of crime, hooliganism or unwanted intrusions into privacy. These require various community provisions, but even more, attention to a number of quite mundane details: for example, flats and houses should be constructed in such a way that the chance of noise annoying neighbours is minimised. Along with these, is the obvious, although often forgotten, need for a positive effort on the part of each individual to think of the effects of his actions upon others, and for willingness to refrain from what is likely to annoy.

Last, and most fundamental, is the need to find new goals for endeavour, which can catch the individual's imagination and co-ordinate his life into a broader pattern. In this way, inevitable constraints and difficulties, that would loom large on their own, can be seen in a wider perspective, and accepted as necessary means towards larger and more worthwhile ends.

It is this last requirement that has traditionally been the special concern of Christianity, but there is a sense in which all the others should concern it also, since all have to do with aspects of the fundamental nature of man, and his place in society and the world. It seems fair to argue, indeed, that the Church needs, if it is to do its work fully, to take an interest in a wider range of factors affecting the quality of life than it has done in the past, including not only values and ideals, individual and social relations, physical and mental health, but everything that makes life satisfying, or that helps man to live his life in a way which expresses to the full what we have called basic reality.

Chapter VIII

Christian Priorities

LOOKING back over the preceding chapters, we can see that they provide a number of pointers for present-day Christian living and for the future work of the Church. We shall here, by way of conclusion, survey briefly what appear to be some of the most important of them.

We have argued that the fundamental Christian task is to live in accordance with the basic realities of the natural world that we can envisage as lying behind the varied events of daily life. We could equally have said that the task is to live *actively* and *enthusiastically* in accordance with *truth*. This is the principle from which all other Christian aims, duties and worthwhile activities derive. It involves three main lines of endeavour, both for Christians as individuals and for the Church as a body: first, the discovery of truth; second, the taking of outgoing action in the service of the world; and third, the building of a stable and effective Christian society. We shall look at each of these in turn.

Search for truth

It follows from what has just been said, that the first duty of a Christian is to obtain an informed and balanced view of all the issues upon which he is called to make decisions, especially those of a controversial nature. To do this thoroughly, reviewing the whole of the evidence available, distinguishing truth from error and recognising areas of doubt would, of course, be a formidable task, and far beyond the capabilities of any one individual who had his daily work to do, and family responsibilities to discharge. Individual Christians can be expected to take a lively interest in events around them, and to be receptive as well as critical in their approach to new ideas, but they cannot think through all the detailed information on which their decisions need to be based. It seems, therefore, that a Church organisation is needed, to be responsible for gathering and sifting information on all important issues. The organisation's task would not be merely to interpret the Bible, but to appraise, balance and synthesise the best knowledge available, and to make the results known to the world, outlining the evidence, making clear where doubt exists, and spelling out reasons for decisions and policies. Its conclusions would inevitably take sides in many controversial issues, but would need to be unaligned with any political party or sectional interest, and patently unbiassed, even if matters which affected the interests of the Church itself were being considered.

Examples of what such a Church organisation might do include looking objectively and unsentimentally at family problems, especially the role of parents in the upbringing of children, and policies for the care of the aged; examining the human problems that result from large-scale organisation; and formulating methods of restraining the world's population growth. In all cases its work should be to produce positive proposals, and not merely to put forward bare facts or indications of what should *not* be done: for instance, it would not be enough for it to indicate that racial tensions exist in certain areas, and to deplore them; it should instead seek reasons for these tensions, and suggest the courses of action most likely to resolve them.

This would be a difficult task, and would require the recruitment of some very high-grade intellects to form a substantial research team, including not only theologians but also psychologists, economists and experts from industry, social welfare, education, medicine and a number of other areas. The team would be expensive, and it may well be asked whether the work could not be done better in the universities. Unfortunately many of these have largely surrendered the objectivity they once prized, in favour of political action. In any case, the work would be incompatible with any substantial teaching commitments. If such a team did its work well, and the world could rely on its statements always being scrupulously fair, its authority would be immense, and its influence, both individually and socially, would far outreach that of anything the Church does at present.

In the dark ages after the fall of the Roman Empire, the Church was the main guardian and preserver of truth. The rapid expansion of factual knowledge, with all its seeming conflicts, and political and other pressures tending to distort interpretation, make the Church's guardianship of truth even more necessary today. It seems fair to urge that the Church could well put a very substantial portion of its best resources into such work, and that if it did so, it would gain far greater support than it has had for a long time.

Service to the world

Christians and the Church need not only to discover the truth but, when they have found it, to propagate it and act on it carefully yet vigorously and decisively. For the individual, the largest part of this action will obviously consist of doing his daily work, and taking his part in his family, enthusiastically and to the very best of his ability. It will also involve him in concern for wider issues, which will include taking some share in the un-paid work of the community, thinking carefully about problems of the day, and exercising his voting rights in the support of those policies which he judges to be the most honest, realistic, far-sighted and in accord with the genuine needs of man. At the same time, in order to maintain his capacity to carry out all these activities well, he should take an adequate measure of rest, recreation and holiday, enjoying them without any feeling that they imply a dereliction of duty.

The Church as a body can be justly proud of its record of action in many types of service to the world, especially in education, medicine, and social welfare. Schools, hospitals and relief organisations all owe their beginnings to work by the Church or by individual members of it, not only in developed Christian countries, but also through missionaries working in less advanced areas. Missionary activities have sometimes been rightly criticised for having unthinkingly tried to substitute European social patterns for previously existing ones which were better suited to the people concerned, and for having thus unnecessarily disturbed their stability of life. Mission schools and hospitals, however, set standards which no secular body would have achieved, so that it was men trained in mission schools who made it possible for many of the countries in Asia and Africa to attain independence, and hospitals with a mission background still tend to be far superior to others in those continents.

It is a measure of the Church's success, that in almost every country, old and new, most of this work has now been taken over by state agencies. These can deploy vastly greater resources than the Church can muster, and thus leave the Church with the choice of continuing to play an appreciable, although secondary role, or of finding new directions in which to turn its attention. It seems a waste of the Church's resources, and inappropriate to its aims, that it should merely act as a subsidiary to the state: if the Church is concerned with the discovery and propagation of the truth, its proper role is to lead and to pioneer. It should be at the forefront of any new studies not only in education, medicine and social work, but also in corrective penal treatment, conservation of the natural environment, town planning, industrial work and human relationships generally — in short, in any area where decisions have to be taken in the light of knowledge about the fundamental nature of man. Its aim, however, should not be to claim exclusive rights in any of these areas, but rather to show the way to secular bodies, and to hand over to them once standards have been established. Its part may not only involve direct action in, for example, running an experimental school or hospital; but may also take the form of stimulating research and the appraisal of new ideas, or of pressing for more humane and efficient methods of organisation.

The motives behind the establishment of church schools, hospitals and welfare agencies in the past has been, in part, straightforwardly humanitarian, and in part the creation of vehicles for propagating Christian ideas. The second of these motives has sometimes been regarded as sufficient in itself, but it is not so if the role we have suggested here for the Church is accepted. The church school should not be just an ordinary school which includes more religious instruction in its syllabus than other schools: it should all the time be pioneering, for example in methods of teaching designed to bring out the best in children of different personalities, temperaments and backgrounds, with a view to showing state schools the way to better education. The church hospital should not be just an ordinary hospital with a greater than normal provision of chaplaincy services: it should be continually reaching forward, say by devising and testing methods of treating people more humanely, and acting as a model to secular hospitals in such matters as politeness of staff, arrangements to avoid long periods of waiting by out-patients, and the efficient deployment of human and technical resources.

In all these various activities, individual Christians and the Church as a body are likely to find themselves involved from time to time in political issues. It is sometimes held that, because of this, the Church should form a political party, and in several countries certain denominations are indeed associated with particular parties. If, however, the Church's essential task is to find, propagate and act upon truth, it is a negation of this task if it engages in the compromises, biassed statements, half-truths and distortions of fact that seem to be virtually essential for any political party which, at least in the present climate of opinion, hopes to gain, and keep power. In any case, the assumption of political power would lay the Church open to the temptation of substituting the force of law for the persuasion of truth. The Church's political role seems not to be that of a party, but of scrutinising legislation, of bringing to the notice of both politicians and public the truth behind political issues, and of pressing for these to be decided on their merits in a far-sighted manner, rather than for the advantage of any sectional interest. Such action by the Church would, in the long run, give it a far more important and influential role than that of a party, and its injection of sobering truth into political debate could be a powerful means of fostering higher standards of political integrity.

The Christian society

In the preceding discussion, the Church has been regarded as the agent of Christianity in the discovery of truth and the taking of action in the world. In Chapter V we outlined its other major role as a society, in which individual Christians can find the means of learning and keeping in mind Christian ideas, engage in joint activities within a group of like-minded companions, and have opportunities of putting Christian values and ideals into practice on a scale such that each individual can make a significant contribution. Looked at from a psychological point of view, the Church is therefore an organisation with problems of matching its activities to the needs and capacities of its members, and of securing effective leadership in a hierarchical structure.

If the needs of different people are to be adequately matched, there must be, as mentioned in Chapter V, variety in church services and other activities. Just what characteristics of services and activities are appropriate for different people is still, however, far from certain, and is one aspect of a more general ignorance. The parish clergyman has no well-documented body of knowledge to guide him on practical matters which is comparable with those available to almost every other profession. As a result, every newly ordained clergyman has to start virtually from scratch in building up his techniques of dealing with people, and organising and guiding his church's activities. Little wonder that many parish activities seem to be trivial exercises, ministering to demands for attention made by small-minded people, repudiated by most of the more able members as they grow through adolescence to the attainment of a wider view of the world, making the Church and its work often appear pathetic in the eyes of better-founded professions, and generally setting a premium on mediocrity.

To remedy this deficiency, two developments appear to be required. First, there is a need for a body of qualified people to collect, and write down, the experience gained by the more insightful clergy and laymen in a wide variety of parishes and over a wide range of church activities. Such a body would be likely to find a number of striking uniformities which could serve as the immediate basis of manuals for future clergy and parish workers. Equally, they are likely to find some wide discrepancies between the experiences of different people and in different places. These discrepancies should be the starting points of carefully controlled research, to ascertain why particular practices have been successful, and to define the circumstances in which each is best followed.

Second, there is a need for improved training of clergy. Many — perhaps most — present clergy training colleges concentrate on the development of devotional life, together with some elementary theology and a sketchy practical instruction. The results are often unfortunate: many men who have been sound, even brilliant, university students seem to come out of theological colleges with their intellects blunted and their vision blurred. The trained clergyman should be a high-grade professional, capable of earning the respect of medical practitioners, psychiatrists, teachers, social workers, industrial managers, trade-union leaders and politicians, and able to ask penetrating questions of scientists, economists and historians, even if he does not have the knowledge to meet them on their own ground. He should be accurately informed about current affairs and free from political bias, he should be worthy of the confidence of others and know how to gain and keep it, and should be able to teach simply and lucidly, especially to the more intelligent and critical adults and adolescents in his parish. The quality of man needed for such training is high, but studies of leadership made in many different situations agree that effective leaders are almost always more able, knowledgeable, responsible, adaptable and generally active than those they lead (for a summary see Gibb, 1969). It is perhaps fair to suggest that really first-rate professional training for clergy would attract men of the calibre needed to profit from it.

PRIEST AND PROPHET

The history of Christianity, and of the Judaism that preceded it, has been of an interplay between the priest, who has been the maintainer of tradition and the preserver of order, and the prophet who has been the man of new ideas, the reformer who looks away from what has been and is now, to what might and ought to be in the future. Both have been necessary. Without the priest, Judaism and Christianity would have long ago been dispersed, and their ideas lost, in the comings and goings of events. Without the prophet, they would have been static, drifting further and further out of touch with the needs of their times. Typically, it has been the priest who has been the builder and guardian of the Church as an organised society, and the prophet who has stimulated that society into action in relation to the outside world, and who has been the searcher for new insights into truth.

In recent years, the Church appears to have been dominated by men who, with one or two notable exceptions, have had priestly aims. It is true that there have been innovations such as new church services and revised translations of the Bible. These, however, are trivial changes within a system of doctrine that has remained essentially unchanged. The leading prophets of modern days have been secular advocates of political systems or moral ideas, which leave Christianity aside even if they are not actually hostile to it. The time seems to have come when the prophet needs to be brought back into the forefront of the Church's work.

A modern Christian prophet would probably not be a man like John the Baptist, living rough as he thundered his message of doom, nor would he be a purveyor of panaceas such as transcendental meditation or of catch phrases such as "personal devotion to a personal saviour." Instead he would almost certainly be a man of incisive intellect, with a capacity for hard work, well trained, sophisticated, insightful, persuasive, able to hold his own with the best brains of the day in other walks of life, respecting tradition but not hidebound by it any more than he would be hidebound by the idea of change for change's sake. Above all, he would be a fearless seeker after truth, looking afresh at the fundamental aims, doctrines and practices of Christianity and the Church, bringing them into line with the vast store of modern knowledge we now possess about man and his world, and making Christian ideas understandable by those who, for reasons of background or education, have no contact with them at present. The work of men such as this could indeed enable Christianity and the Church to play the part envisaged for them in the New Testament, and give the Christian society an effectiveness greater than it has ever had before.

References

Adler, A. (1938) *Social Interest*. London: Faber & Faber.

Adorno, T. W., Frenkel-Brunswik, E., Levinson, D. J. & Sanford, R. N. (1950) *The Authoritarian Personality*. London: Harper & Row.

Allport, G. W. (1951) *The Individual and his Religion*. London: Constable.

Allport, G. W. (1954) *The Nature of Prejudice*. Cambridge, Mass.: Addison-Wesley.

Allport, G. W. & Kramer, B. M. (1946) Some roots of prejudice. *J. Psychol.*, *22*, 9-39.

Allport, G. W. & Ross, J. M. (1967) Personal religious orientation and prejudice. *J. Person. Soc. Psychol.*, *5*, 432-443.

Anderson, C. C. (1962) A developmental study of dogmatism during adolescence with reference to sex differences. *J. Abnorm. Soc. Psychol.*, *65*, 132-135.

Argyle, M. (1958) *Religious Behaviour*. London: Routledge & Kegan Paul.

Argyle, M. (1961) Psychological research into the origins of the conscience. *Modern Churchman*, *5*, 50-58.

Argyle, M. & Delin, P. (1965) Non-universal laws of socialization. *Human Relations*, *18*, 77-86.

Aronfreed, J. (1961) The nature, variety and social patterning of moral responses to transgression. *J. Abnorm. Soc. Psychol.*, *63*, 223-240.

Aronson, E. & Carlsmith, J. M. (1963) Effect of the severity of threat on the devaluation of forbidden behavior. *J. Abnorm. Soc. Psychol.*, *66*, 584-588.

Bartlett, F. C. (1932) *Remembering*. Cambridge University Press.

Bartlett, F. C. (1950) *Religion as Experience, Belief, Action*. (Riddell Memorial Lectures). Oxford University Press.

Battle, Esther S. (1965) Motivational determinants of academic task persistence. *J. Person. Soc. Psychol.*, *2*, 209–218.

Belbin, Eunice. (1964) *Training the Adult Worker*. D.S.I.R. Problems of Progress in Industry No. 15. London: H.M.S.O.

Belbin, R. M. (1965) *Training Methods for Older Workers*. Paris: O.E.C.D.

Belbin, R. M. (1969) *The Discovery Method*: *an International Experiment in Retraining*. Paris: O.E.C.D.

Bell, H. M. (1938) *Youth Tell their Story*. New York: Amer. Coun. Educ.

Bender, I. E. (1958) Changes in religious interest: a retest after 15 years. *J. Abnorm. Soc. Psychol.*, *57*, 41–46.

Bethlehem, D. W. (1969) Guilt, self-ideal discrepancy, the approval motive and recollections of socialization: some interrelationships. *Brit. J. Soc. Clin. Psychol.*, *8*, 323–332.

Birren, J. E. (1965) Age changes in speed of behavior: its central nature and physiological correlates. In: *Behavior, Aging and the Nervous System*, (Ed. A. T. Welford & J. E. Birren). Springfield, Illinois: Charles C. Thomas.

Black, M. S. & London, P. (1966) The dimensions of guilt, religion and personal ethics. *J. Soc. Psychol.*, *69*, 39–54.

Blackburn, R. (1969) Sensation seeking, impulsivity and psychopathic personality. *J. Consult. Clin. Psychol.*, *33*, 571–574.

Blum, Barbara S. & Mann, J. H. (1960) The effect of religious membership on religious prejudice. *J. Soc. Psychol.*, *52*, 97–101.

Brim, O. G. & Hoff, D. B. (1957) Individual and situational differences in desire for certainty. *J. Abnorm. Soc. Psychol.*, *54*, 225–229.

Brock, T. C. (1963) Effects of prior dishonesty on post-decision dissonance. *J. Abnorm. Soc. Psychol.*, *66*, 325–331.

Brock, T. C. & Becker, L. A. (1967) Volition and attraction in everyday life. *J. Soc. Psychol.*, *72*, 89–97.

Broen, W. E. (1957) A factor-analytic study of religious attitudes. *J. Abnorm. Soc. Psychol.*, *54*, 176–179.

Brown, D. G. & Lowe, W. L. (1951) Religious beliefs and personality characteristics of college students. *J. Soc. Psychol.*, *33*, 103–129.

Brown, L. B. (1962) A study of religious belief. *Brit. J. Psychol.*, *53*, 259–272.

REFERENCES

Brown, L. B. (1965) Aggression and denominational membership. *Brit. J. Soc. Clin. Psychol.*, *4*, 175–178.

Brown, L. B. (1966) Egocentric thought in petitionary prayer: a cross-cultural study. *J. Soc. Psychol.*, *68*, 197–210.

Brown, L. B. (1968) Some attitudes underlying petitionary prayer. In *From Cry to Word*. 'Lumen Vitae' Studies in Religious Psychology. pp. 455–474.

Brown, L. B. (1969) Confirmation and religious belief. *Victoria University of Wellington Publications in Psychology. No. 22.*

Brown, L. B. & Thouless, R. H. (1965) Animistic thought in civilized adults. *J. Genet. Psychol.*, *107*, 33–42.

Burkitt, F. C. (1932) *Jesus Christ*. London: Blackie & Son.

Burnstein, E. & McRae, A. V. (1962) Some effects of shared threat and prejudice in racially mixed groups. *J. Abnorm. Soc. Psychol.*, *64*, 257–263.

Clark, E. T. (1937) *The Small Sects in America*. Nashville, Tenn.: Cokesbury.

Clark, W. H. (1955) A study of some of the factors leading to achievement and creativity, with special reference to religious scepticism and belief. *J. Soc. Psychol.*, *41*, 57–69.

Cline, V. B. & Richards, J. M. (1965) A factor-analytic study of religious belief and behavior. *J. Person. Soc. Psychol.*, *1*, 569–578.

Cooley, C. E. & Hutton, J. B. (1965) Adolescent response to religious appeal as related to IPAT anxiety. *J. Soc. Psychol.*, *67*, 325–327.

Dreger, R. M. (1952) Some personality correlates of religious attitudes, as determined by projective techniques. *Psychol. Monog.*, *66*, No. 3.

Eisenman, R. (1967) Sex differences in moral judgement. *Percept. Mot. Skills*, *24*, 784.

Engel, G. (1968) Some college students' responses concerning negroes of differing religious background. *J. Soc. Psychol.*, *74*, 275–283.

Farley, F. & Farley, Sonja V. (1967) Extroversion and stimulus-seeking motivation. *J. Consult. Psychol.*, *31*, 215–216.

Flower, J. C. (1927) *The Psychology of Religion*. London: Kegan Paul.

Freedman, J. L., Wallington, Sue A. & Bless, Evelyn. (1967) Compliance without pressure: the effect of guilt. *J. Person. Soc. Psychol.*, *7*, 117–124.

Freud, S. (1916) History of the psychoanalytic movement. *Psychoanal. Rev.*, *3*, 406–454.

Freud, S. (1919) *Totem and Taboo*. London: Kegan Paul.

Freud, S. (1928) *The Future of an Illusion*. London: Hogarth Press.

Freud, S. (1933) *New Introductory Lectures on Psycho-Analysis*. New York: W. W. Norton & Co.

Galton, F. (1908) *Memories of my Life*. London: Methuen.

Garrison, K. C. (1962) The relationship of certain variables to church-sect typology among college students. *J. Soc. Psychol.*, *56*, 29–32.

Gibb, C. A. (Ed.) (1969) *Leadership*. Harmondsworth: Penguin Books.

Gibbs, C. B. & Brown, I. D. (1956) Increased production from information incentives in an uninteresting repetitive task. *Manager*, *24*, 374–379.

Gibson, J. J. (1950) *The Perception of the Visual World*. Boston, Mass.: Houghton Mifflin.

Gilbert, Jeanne, G. & Lombardi, D. N. (1967) Personality characteristics of young male narcotic addicts. *J. Consult. Psychol.*, *31*, 536–538.

Gilliland, A. R. (1953) Changes in religious beliefs of college students. *J. Soc. Psychol.*, *37*, 113–116.

Godin, A. & van Roey, Bernadette. (1959) Immanent justice and divine protection in children of 6 to 14 years. *Lumen Vitae*, *14*, 129–148.

Goldstein, M. J., Rodnick, E. H., Judd, L. L. & Gould, E. (1970) Galvanic skin reactivity among family groups containing disturbed adolescents. *J. Abnorm. Psychol.*, *75*, 57–67.

Greenfield, N. S. (1959) The relationship between recalled forms of childhood discipline and psychopathology. *J. Consult. Psychol.*, *23*, 139–142.

Gregory, R. L. (1966) *Eye and Brain: the Psychology of Seeing*. London: World University Library.

Gregory, W. E. (1957) The orthodoxy of the authoritarian personality. *J. Soc. Psychol.*, *45*, 217–232.

Grim, P. F., Kohlberg, L. & White, S. H. (1968) Some relationships between conscience and attentional processes. *J. Person. Soc. Psychol.*, *8*, 239–252.

Grimble, A. (1953) *A Pattern of Islands*. London: Murray.

Grusec, Joan. (1966) Some antecedents of self-criticism. *J. Person. Soc. Psychol.*, *4*, 244–252.

Haan, Norma, Smith, M. B. & Block, Jeanne. (1968) Moral reasoning of young adults: political-social behaviour, family background and personality correlates. *J. Person. Soc. Psychol.*, *10*, 183–201.

Haimes, P. & Hetherington, Mavis. (1964) Attitudes of the clergy toward behavior problems of children. *J. Soc. Psychol.*, *62*, 329–334.

Harms, E. (1944) The development of religious experience in children. *Amer. J. Sociol.*, *50*, 112–122.

Havens, J. (1964) A study of religious conflict in college students. *J. Soc. Psychol.*, *64*, 77–87.

Hebb, D. O. (1955) Drives and the C.N.S. (Conceptual Nervous System). *Psychol. Rev.*, *62*, 243–254.

Hites, R. W. (1965) Change in religious attitudes during four years of college. *J. Soc. Psychol.*, *66*, 51–63.

Hocking, J. & Robertson, M. (1969) Sensation seeking scale as a predictor of need for stimulation during sensory restriction. *J. Consult. Clin. Psychol.*, *33*, 367–369.

Hoffman, M. L. & Saltzstein, H. D. (1967) Parent discipline and the child's moral development. *J. Person. Soc. Psychol.*, *5*, 45–57.

Huxley, A. (1954) *The Doors of Perception.* London: Chatto & Windus.

Jahoda, G. (1958) Child animism: II a study in West Africa. *J. Soc. Psychol.*, *47*, 213–222.

James, W. (1902) *The Varieties of Religious Experience.* New York: Longmans, Green & Co.

Jaques, E. (1956) *Measurement of Responsibility.* London: Tavistock Publications.

Jeeves, M. A. (1959) Contribution on prejudice and religion and general statement on nature and purpose of religious psychology. In: *Proceedings of the Fifteenth International Congress of Psychology. Brussels* – 1957. Amsterdam: North Holland Publishing Co. pp. 508–510.

Johnson, P. E. (1953) *Psychology of Pastoral Care.* Nashville, Tenn.: Abingdon Press.

Jones, M. B. (1958) Religious values and authoritarian tendency. *J. Soc. Psychol.*, *48*, 83–89.

Jourard, S. M. (1954) Moral indignation: a correlate of denied dislike of parents' traits. *J. Consult. Psychol.*, *18*, 59–60.

Jung, C. G. (1933) *Psychology of the Unconscious*. London: Kegan Paul, Trench, Trubner & Co.

Jung, C. G. (1938) *Psychology and Religion*. New Haven, Conn.: Yale University Press.

Kallmann, F. J. (1953) *Heredity in Health and Mental Disorder*. New York: Norton.

Kallmann, F. J. (1957) Twin data on the genetics of ageing. In: *Ciba Foundation Colloquia on Ageing, Vol. 3*. (Ed. G. E. W. Wolstenholme & Cecelia M. O'Connor). London: Churchill, pp. 131–143.

Kawwa, T. (1968) A survey of ethnic attitudes of some British secondary school pupils. *Brit. J. Soc. Clin. Psychol., 7*, 161–168.

Kimber, J. A. M. (1947) Interests and personality traits of Bible institute students. *J. Soc. Psychol., 26*, 225–233.

Kimble, G. A. (1961) *Hilgard & Marquis' Conditioning & Learning*. New York: Appleton-Century-Crofts.

Kish, G. B. & Busse, W. (1968) Correlates of stimulus-seeking: age, education, intelligence and aptitudes. *J. Consult. Clin. Psychol., 32*, 633–637.

Kleemeier, R. W. (1951) The effect of a work program on adjustment attitudes in an aged population. *J. Gerontol., 6*, 372–379.

Klinger, E., Albaum, Anita & Hetherington, Mavis. (1964) Factors influencing the severity of moral judgements. *J. Soc. Psychol., 63*, 319–326.

Leff, R. (1969) Effects of punishment intensity and consistency on the internalization of behavioral suppression in children. *Develop. Psychol., 1*, 345–356.

Leuba, J. H. (1912) *A Psychological Study of Religion*. New York: Macmillan.

Lewis, M. (1965) Psychological effect of effort. *Psychol. Bull., 64*, 183–190.

London, P., Schulman, R. E. & Black, M. S. (1964) Religion, guilt and ethical standards. *J. Soc. Psychol., 63*, 145–159.

Lowe, W. L. (1954) Group beliefs and socio-cultural factors in religious delusions. *J. Soc. Psychol., 40*, 267–274.

McCann, R. V. (1959) An empirical study of religious change. In: *Proceedings of the Fifteenth International Congress of Psychology. Brussels – 1957*. Amsterdam: North Holland Publishing Co. pp. 510–511.

McConnell, T. R. (1963) Suggestibility in children as a function of chronological age. *J. Abnorm. Soc. Psychol.*, *67*, 286–289.

McCord, Joan, McCord, W. & Thurber, Emily. (1962) Some effects of paternal absence on male children. *J. Abnorm. Soc. Psychol.*, *64*, 361–369.

MacKenzie, Barbara K. (1948) The importance of contact in determining attitudes toward negroes. *J. Abnorm. Soc. Psychol.*, *43*, 417–441.

MacRae, D. (1954) A test of Piaget's theories of moral development. *J. Abnorm. Soc. Psychol.*, *49*, 14–18.

Martin, C. & Nichols, R. C. (1962) Personality and religious belief. *J. Soc. Psychol.*, *56*, 3–8.

Martin, D. & Wrightsman, L. S. (1965) The relationship between religious behavior and concern about death. *J. Soc. Psychol.*, *65*, 317–323.

Meadow, A. & Bronson, Louise. (1969) Religious affiliation and psychopathology in a Mexican-American population. *J. Abnorm. Psychol.*, *74*, 177–180.

Mischel, W. (1961) Preference for delayed reinforcement and social responsibility. *J. Abnorm. Soc. Psychol.*, *62*, 1–7.

Mischel, W., Grusec, Joan, & Masters, J. C. (1969) Effects of expected delay time on the subjective value of rewards and punishments. *J. Person. Soc. Psychol.*, *11*, 363–373.

Mischel, W. & Metzner, R. (1962) Preference for delayed reward as a function of age, intelligence and length of delay interval. *J. Abnorm. Soc. Psychol.*, *64*, 425–431.

Moberg, D. O. (1956) Religious activities and personal adjustment in old age. *J. Soc. Psychol.*, *43*, 261–267.

Moulton, R. W., Liberty, P. G. Burnstein, E. & Altucher, N. (1966) Patterning of parental affection and disciplinary dominance as a determinant of guilt and sex typing. *J. Person. Soc. Psychol*, *4*, 356–363.

Mull, Helen K. (1947) A comparison of religious thinking of freshmen and seniors in a liberal arts college. *J. Soc. Psychol.*, *26*, 121–123.

Newcomb, T. M. & Svehla, G. (1937) Intra-family relationships in attitude. *Sociometry*, *1*, 180–205.

Nowlan, E. H. (1957) The picture of the 'Catholic' which emerges from attitude tests. *Lumen Vitae*, *12*, 275–285.

O'Reilly, C. T. & O'Reilly, E. J. (1954) Religious beliefs of Catholic college students and their attitudes toward minorities. *J. Abnorm. Soc. Psychol.*, *49*, 378–380.

Pan, Ju-Shu. (1952) A comparison of factors in the personal adjustment of old people in the Protestant Church homes for the aged and old people living outside of institutions. *J. Soc. Psychol.*, *35*, 195–203.

Philp, H. L. (1956) *Freud and Religious Belief.* London: Rockcliff Publishing Corporation.

Piaget, J. (1932) *The Moral Judgement of the Child.* London: Kegan Paul, Trench & Trubner.

Poppleton, Pamela K. & Pilkington, G. W. (1963) The measurement of religious attitudes in a university population. *Brit. J. Soc. Clin. Psychol.*, *2*, 20–36.

Reichard, Suzanne, Livson, Florine & Petersen, P. G. (1962) *Aging and Personality.* New York: John Wiley & Sons.

Ruma, Eleanor H. & Mosher, D. L. (1967) Relationship between moral judgement and guilt in delinquent boys. *J. Abnorm. Psychol.*, *72*, 122–127.

Sears, R. R., Maccoby, E. E. & Levin, H. (1957) *Patterns of Child Rearing.* New York: Row, Peterson & Co.

Shapiro, D. S. (1957) Perceptions of significant family and environmental relationships in aggressive and withdrawn children. *J. Consult. Psychol.*, *21*, 381–385.

Shippee-Blum, Eva M. (1959) The young rebel: self-regard and ego-ideal. *J. Consult. Psychol.*, *23*, 44–50.

Sollenberger, R. T. (1968) Chinese-American child-rearing practices and juvenile delinquency. *J. Soc. Psychol.*, *74*, 13–23.

Starbuck, E. D. (1899) *The Psychology of Religion.* London: Walter Scott.

Stewart, L. & Livson, N. (1966) Smoking and rebelliousness: a longitudinal study from childhood to maturity. *J. Consult. Psychol.*, *30*, 225–229.

Telford, C. W. (1950) A study of religious attitudes. *J. Soc. Psychol.*, *31*, 217–230.

Thouless, R. H. (1923) *An Introduction to the Psychology of Religion.* Cambridge University Press.

Thouless, R. H. (1935) The tendency to certainty in religious belief. *Brit. J. Psychol.*, *26*, 16–31.

REFERENCES

Thouless, R. H. (1940) *Conventionalization and Assimilation in Religious Movements.* (Riddell Memorial Lectures). Oxford University Press.

Thouless, R. H. (1959) Psychologie und Religion. In *Handbuch der Psychologie: 2 Auflage* (Ed. D. Katz). Basel: Benno Schwabe.

Thouless, R. H. & Brown, L. B. (1964) Petitionary prayer: belief in its appropriateness and causal efficacy among adolescent girls. In: *From Religious Experience to a Religious Attitude.* Studies in Religious Psychology–III. Brussels: International Centre for Studies in Religious Education. pp. 123–136.

Townsend, P. (1957) *The Family Life of Old People.* London: Routledge & Kegan Paul.

Ugurel-Semin, Refia. (1952) Moral behaviour and moral judgement of children. *J. Abnorm. Soc. Psychol.*, 47, 463–474.

Van der Post, L. (1964) *Journey into Russia.* London: Hogarth Press.

Ward, C. D. & Barrett, J. E. (1968) The Ecumenical Council and attitude change among Catholic, Protestant and Jewish college students. *J. Soc. Psychol.*, 74, 91–96.

Watson, J. D. (1968) *The Double Helix.* London: Weidenfeld & Nicolson.

Weatherhead, L. D. (1929) *Psychology in Service of the Soul.* London: Epworth Press.

Weatherley, D. (1962) Maternal permissiveness toward aggression and subsequent TAT aggression. *J. Abnorm. Soc. Psychol.*, 65, 1–5.

Welford, A. T. (1946) An attempt at an experimental approach to the psychology of religion. *Brit. J. Psychol.*, 36, 55–73.

Welford, A. T. (1947a) Is religious behavior dependent upon affect or frustration? *J. Abnorm. Soc. Psychol.*, 42, 310–319.

Welford, A. T. (1947b) A psychological footnote to prayer. *Theology Today*, 3, 498–501.

Welford, A. T. (1948) The use of archaic language in religious expression: an example of 'canalized response'. *Brit. J. Psychol.*, 38, 209–217.

Welford, A. T. (1959) On the measurement of religious attitude and behaviour. In: *Proceedings of the Fifteenth International Congress of Psychology. Brussels – 1957.* Amsterdam: North Holland Publishing Co. pp. 506–508.

Welford, A. T. (1965) Stress and achievement. *Austral. J. Psychol.*, *17*, 1–11.

Welford, A. T. (1966) Individual capacity and social demands: a new look at social psychology. In: *Operational Research and the Social Sciences* (Ed. J. R. Lawrence). London: Tavistock Publications. pp. 531–542.

Welford, A. T. (1968) *Fundamentals of Skill.* London: Methuen.

Wicker, A. W. (1969) Size of church membership and members' support of church behavior settings. *J. Person. Soc. Psychol.*, *13*, 278–288.

Williams, R. L. & Cole, S. (1968) Religiosity, generalized anxiety and apprehension concerning death. *J. Soc. Psychol.*, *75*, 111–117.

Wilson, W. C. (1960) Extrinsic religious values and prejudice. *J. Abnorm. Soc. Psychol.*, *60*, 286–288.

Woodworth, R. S. (1958) *Dynamics of Behavior.* New York: Henry Holt & Co. London: Methuen.

Wright, D. & Cox, E. (1967a) Religious belief and co-education in a sample of sixth-form boys and girls. *Brit. J. Soc. Clin. Psychol.*, *6*, 23–31.

Wright, D. & Cox, E. (1967b) A study of the relationship between moral judgement and religious belief in a sample of English adolescents. *J. Soc. Psychol.*, *72*, 135–144.

Yaryan, Ruby B. & Festinger, L. (1961) Preparatory action and belief in the probable occurrence of future events. *J. Abnorm. Soc. Psychol.*, *63*, 603–606.

Zuckerman, Marvin, Kolin, Elizabeth A., Price, Leah & Zoob, Ina. (1964) Development of a sensation-seeking scale. *J. Consult, Psychol.*, *28*, 477–482.

Index

ability, 16, 22, 41, 134, 137, 138, 161, 165
Adler, A., 20, 37, 38, 43
adolescence, 23, 25, 34, 87, 115, 116, 121, 148, 164
Adorno, T. W., 45
affluence, 159–61
after-life, 71, 80
aggression, 104, 119, 164
alienation, 87
Allport, G. W., 21, 45 et seq.
Anderson, C. C., 26
anxiety, 43, 45, 65, 74, 88, 116, 117, 157
Argyle, M., 21, 33, 40, 45, 61, 81 et seq., 104
Aronfreed, J., 81
Aronson, E., 75
arousal, 94, 141, 142
attitudes, 13, 23, 25, 45, 127, 152
authoritarianism, 45, 47, 104

Barrett, J. E., 83, 187
Bartlett, F. C., 38, 39, 43, 52, 64
"basic reality", 56, 58, 84, 98, 167, 168
Battle, E. S., 162
Becker, L. A., 162
behaviour, Christian, 90, 148, 168–77
Belbin, E., 150
Belbin, R. M., 150
belief, 22–24, 39, 41, 89, 91
Bell, H. M., 34
Bender, I. E., 24, 25
Bethlehem, D. W., 82
Bible, 25, 28, 29, 46, 91, 97–99, 102, 103, 128, 130, 151, 176; new translations, 58, 101; New Testament, 64, 88, 177; Old Testament, 51, 98
Birren, J. E., 155
birth control, 25, 46, 47, 114, 144

Black, M. S., 83
Blackburn, R., 159
Blum, B. S., 45
boredom, 14, 124, 159, 160
brain, 12, 15, 23, 48, 52, 62, 133, 146, 147, 153, 155
Brim, O. G., 89
Brock, T. C., 83, 162
Broen, W. E., 46
Bronson, L., 44
Brown, D. G., 24, 25, 45
Brown, I. D., 76
Brown, L. B., 26, 45, 54, 90, 104
Burkitt, F. C., 69
Burnstein, E., 135
Busse, W., 160

Carlsmith, J. M., 75
Charcot, J. M., 113
children, *see* family
church as Body of Christ, 92; as a social group, 92–97, 168; attendances, 24, 25; services, 29, 31, 87, 94, 95, 97, 99–102, 106; union, 105–8
Church of England, 31, 93, 104; Prayer Book, 42, 60, 99–102, 112
Clark, E. T., 40
Clark, W. H., 45
clergy and ministers, 21, 45, 94, 99–101, 107, 174–5
Cline, V. B., 45
coding, 12, 50, 110, 116, 140, 148
Cole, S., 45
communism, 29, 32
compensation, 37, 40, 105
computor analogy, 15, 48–50, 147
conceptual units, 53, 55, 57
confidence, *see* uncertainty
conscience, 61, 81–84, 120
consciousness, 12, 14, 85